COLOR
CONCRETE
GARDEN
PROJECTS

WITHDRAWN

COLOR CONCRETE GARDEN PROJECTS

Make your own planters, furniture, and fire pits using creative techniques and vibrant finishes

NATHAN SMITH & MICHAEL SNYDER

Photographs by
CHARLES COLEMAN

TIMBER PRESS
Portland, Oregon

Frontispiece: Making your own colored concrete projects brings a new level of richness to your garden.

Photos copyright © Charles Coleman except those on page 17 by Jeremy French.

The Haseltine Building
133 S.W. Second Avenue, Suite 450
Portland, Oregon 97204-3527
timberpress.com

Printed in China

Text design by Susan Applegate
Cover design by Patrick Barber

A catalog record for this book is also available from the British Library.

Library of Congress Cataloging-in-Publication Data

Smith, Nathan, 1981-
    Color concrete garden projects : make your own planters, furniture, and fire pits using creative techniques and vibrant finishes / Nathan Smith and Michael Snyder ; photographs by Charles Coleman.
        pages cm
    Includes index.
    ISBN 978-1-60469-539-7
    1. Garden ornaments and furniture--Design and construction. 2. Concrete construction--Formwork. I. Snyder, Michael, 1976- II. Title.
    SB473.5.S624 2015
    721'.0445--dc23   2014048495

TO ALL THOSE WHO ENJOY AND SHARE IN
THE CREATIVE PROCESS AND WHO LIVE TO
PUSH THEMSELVES FURTHER AND GROW
BETTER THAN THEY WERE THE DAY BEFORE

CONTENTS

PREFACE

For as long as we can remember, we've enjoyed making things. Somewhere along the way, making and creating became a part of who we are, and we now feel as though we were made for this sort of work—we find it impossible to get away from. Not only is it a part of who we are, but it continually informs who we are becoming. This is the capacity, benefit, and wonder of creative undertakings. Many people do not see themselves as creative, but we hope this book will encourage everyone to try their hand at making. And working with concrete is a wonderful way to do it. The effort and insight put forth here will, we hope, persuade others to find their creative selves and make creating a part of their daily lives.

At our company, Set in Stone, we are passionate about making beautiful, useful objects and helping others develop richer lives doing the same. We believe that opportunities to apply creativity are invitations to grow as individuals and live deeper, more satisfying lives. By the end of this book not only will you have a variety of beautifully colored concrete pieces for your garden, but you will also have the technical knowledge and confidence to modify and adapt these ideas for your own original projects.

Enjoy!

◄ The projects in this book are an invitation to make personal creative endeavors a way of life.

Nathan and Michael

GETTING CREATIVE WITH CONCRETE
AN INTRODUCTION

Concrete is a simple, beautiful, and very accessible medium with which to explore one's creativity. The process of creation is just that—a process. It is human nature to influence and improve our environment, and the process generally begins with an idea that fills a need, whether that need is functional or aesthetic.

The heart of creative action is problem-solving, and we believe that everyone can do it, although it takes practice. This is exactly what these projects are about—exploring your own methods of problem-solving and making things you love. Everyone can creatively affect their world, and working with colored concrete is a wonderful way to do it.

Once you have determined what it is you want to make, you have to figure out how to make it. There is usually more than one way to go about a project, so take some time at the beginning and weigh the options. Planning is the part most people want to skip—they are eager to jump in, get dirty, and begin making, which is understandable. But spending some time planning can save a lot of pain and frustration in the future. The more time you invest in thinking about the project—where to begin and how to pull it all together—the more original, successful, and enjoyable the project will be. There is always an element of fear here—everyone is afraid of failing. Don't be! The truth is that you are going to fail in some way, but this is something to be embraced and viewed as a learning experience. There is freedom in recognizing you will fail—you'll be inspired to push yourself. With every finished project you will probably have a list of things you would do differently next time. Expect this from the beginning and the journey will be more rewarding. As you work on the projects in this book, your successes and failures will become "concrete" markers that will remind you of how far you've come and of all the lessons learned and frustrations endured.

◄ Creating with our hands gives us richer, more enjoyable lives.

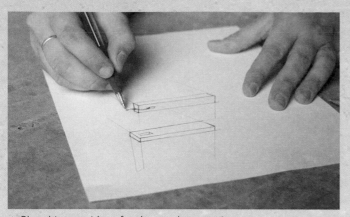

▲ Sketching out ideas for the pendants project.

▲ Playing with the colors for the pendants.

Lemonade out of Lemons

Working in concrete is an engaging and challenging undertaking. A great aspect of decorative concrete is that it is easy to get started with, but challenging enough to warrant interest for years. The intricacies of the craft separate what we do from an everyday sidewalk. We work within much tighter parameters, which means the odds of failure are much greater. These are the times that test your creative fortitude, but you can continue to assess and respond proactively. In the shop we often talk about making lemonade out of lemons. Some of our most distinctive pieces and techniques are the result of working with concrete that did not behave as expected.

Or maybe we just did something stupid. The bench is a good example. We rushed the demolding process (removing the form) and cracked one of the bench's legs because the concrete was still too green. So we embraced our now one-legged bench, gave

▲ An obvious flaw in our cast.

▲ An alternate solution in the form of a prosthetic.

▲ The beauty of imperfection.

it a prosthetic, and moved on. Some people like the bench better this way. All this is just to say, keep your options open and look for unexpected opportunities.

How to Use This Book

Concrete is an amazing medium with which to experiment with color. Not only do we want to challenge and inspire you, we want to give you the understanding to start experimenting on your own, perhaps only using our projects as guidelines or reference. We are all about options because we feel the more options you have in your proverbial tool belt, the more creative and imaginative you can be.

This book is about developing an understanding about color and concrete to a point where you are comfortable creating your own original projects. With only a few exceptions, you can start anywhere in the book—there is no specific order you need to follow other than what keeps you interested. There are several projects that we don't recommend for beginners, but that's because of the carpentry skills needed for building the form. Of course, practice makes perfect, and the more forms you build the easier and more successful they will be, so you'll be able to undertake the complicated forms in no time at all.

CONCRETE FUNDAMENTALS

Concrete is all around us. It is a building block for our cities and infrastructure and is almost so common that we don't recognize it anymore. But this everyday material, typically associated with construction, can be refined into shapes that are beautiful and colorful and even light and delicate. Concrete is essentially high-tech rock. It is resilient, weathers gracefully, and is so aesthetically versatile that you would be hard-pressed to find a more suitable material for the outdoors (or indoors, for that matter). Concrete can be bold and modern, or elegant and subtle, or natural and calming. Achieving these qualities depends on how you use it.

◄ Integral color was used to color this fire pit which is made of three interlocking concrete pieces. One side stores firewood, and the other side has a firebox for the fire.

▲ A concrete chess park.

HOW DOES CONCRETE WORK?

Concrete is a blend of cement, aggregates, and water. To clarify a common misunderstanding, cement is the glue that holds concrete together, while concrete is a combination of cement, aggregates, and water. Aggregates are typically a combination of fine particles, such as sand and larger gravel or crushed rock.

Cement in combination with water acts as the binder, or glue, and aggregates are the filler.

The most widely used cement is Portland cement, which is created by crushing, firing, and finely grinding limestone. When this finely ground powder is combined with water, hydration begins. This chemical process makes the glue that, when blended with various aggregates, creates concrete.

A variety of aggregate sizes or fillers is an important factor in making strong concrete. Imagine a large container full of golf balls. In the container there is a lot of empty space between the individual balls that would have to be filled by glue to hold them all together. All of this space weakens the fundamental structure of concrete. Now imagine filtering smaller marbles and BBs into the container. These small balls would fill up the space between the golf balls and reduce the stress on the glue, thereby strengthening the material. Using various sizes of aggregates reduces the stress on the cement.

Very fine particles called pozzolans are sometimes added to concrete mix designs to help strengthen the chemical structure of con-

▼ The elements of concrete.

1. water
2. pozzolans
3. white Portland cement
4. rock
5. sand
6. gray Portland cement
7. PVA fibers

crete and make a less porous and denser concrete. Pozzolans are silica-rich minerals that are often byproducts of certain industrial processes or naturally mined minerals; some examples include fly ash, silica fume, metakaolin, and VCAS (vitreous calcium aluminosilicate). These minerals are added to a mix and replace a percentage of the cement that goes into a particular mix design. They're found in higher performance mix designs, such as the Buddy Rhodes bagged goods used in some of the projects in this book.

Concrete has strengths and weaknesses. One of concrete's best attributes is its compressive strength—you can place a lot of weight on top of it and not crush it. The flip side is that it has low tensile and flexural strength—it's not very capable of being stretched or bent without breaking apart. It can be reinforced with steel in the form of rebar or ladder wire, or with various types of fibers, to compensate for these shortcomings and give it more tensile and flexural strength.

Adding too much water to cement is the most common mistake made when mixing concrete. Many of the problems experienced with concrete can be traced back to excessive water. As concrete cures, extraneous water evaporates, leaving a poor chemical structure and a certain amount of porosity, shrinkage, and micro cracking. Using only the necessary amount of water is key to successfully mixing concrete.

Numerous chemicals have been

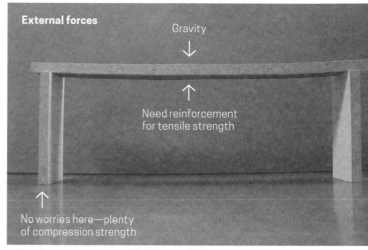

▲ Reinforcement goes in the bottom half.

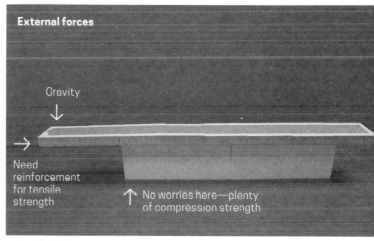

▲ Steel reinforcement goes in the top half.

developed to reduce the amount of water needed to make concrete. These water reducers and plasticizers make the concrete workable and more fluid without compromising the structural strength. Water reducers are used in some of the more refined projects in this book, such as the birdhouse and the dish.

UNDERSTANDING CONCRETE MIXES

While it's important to have a basic understanding of how concrete works, the technical information can be a distraction from the creative process. For that reason, the projects on the following pages rely on a variety of commercial premixes. The convenience of using premixes allows you to pursue concrete as a modern craft rather than chasing the mystery that concrete can sometimes be. The projects in this book use five different bagged mixes, widely available at home-improvement stores or online.

Commercial-Grade Concrete Mixes: Sakrete 5000 Plus Concrete Mix and Quikrete 5000 Concrete Mix

Commercial-grade concrete bagged mixes are available at well-stocked hardware and home-improvement stores. The mixes are preblended and only require the addition of water. Local blenders prepare the mixes so some of the ingredients, mostly the aggregates, will vary by region.

Two common brands are Quikrete and Sakrete. Each brand produces a commercial-grade mix that is formulated for more strength—these are rated as 5000 psi (pounds per square inch). Quikrete 5000 and Sakrete 5000 Plus are the typical industrial gray color associated with concrete. The advantage of these mixes is their ubiquity.

Buddy Rhodes Bone White Concrete Counter Mix

Buddy Rhodes has been a leader in the decorative concrete industry for decades. He developed a unique mix that is more easily controlled by hand, giving his work a handcrafted approach. This mix design is what started Buddy's signature pressed technique: you can take a relatively dry concrete mix and press it by hand not only into the horizontal areas of a form, but also onto the vertical walls of a form. The consistency and workability of the mix allows for numerous finishing options and very professional results. The color of the mix is bone white, which gives you more control over the final color. This mix can be purchased at numerous dealer locations across the country and online.

Buddy Rhodes Bone White Spray Coat

Buddy Rhodes Bone White Spray Coat is an advanced blend of cement, sand, and mineral admixtures (a blend of pozzolans) that results in one of the more versatile and durable base mixes on the market. This mix can be cast, sprayed, placed by hand, carved, and troweled. The fine sands, and the absence of larger aggregates, means the mix can be manipulated to create virtually any finish. We use this mix to pour intricate pieces that are as thin as half an inch. This mix is traditionally reinforced with PVA (polyvinyl alcohol) fibers, and it also has a dry polymer in

► The birdhouse project uses Buddy Rhodes Bone White Spray Coat. Its high-strength properties are perfect for the thin walls and slender curved roof of this piece.

the formula that produces concrete high in both compressive and flexural strength. The color of the mix is bone white, allowing limitless color options. This is a higher performance mix design.

Cheng Pro-Formula Mix

Fu-Tung Cheng is another industry leader. He developed a formula that is added to traditional bagged mixes like Sakrete or Quikrete to give them an ideal balance of performance. By adding Cheng Pro-Formula Mix to a commercial-grade bag of concrete, you can cast stronger and lighter-weight objects than you could with a standard 5000 psi bagged mix alone. Each premeasured bag supplies one cubic foot of mix when combined with 120 pounds of concrete.

Using Cheng Pro-Formula is a good way to get color, water reducer, and other admixtures in one unit. Because of the admixtures in the mix, which give it fluidity and reduce the amount of water needed, this concrete doesn't work well for projects that need finishing or trowelling on the top surface; it is best suited for precast applications or for projects that don't call for finishing the surface. Another caveat is that the mix will usually have a fairly large aggregate; this is fine for some projects but is limiting in finer work. Since Cheng Pro-Formula uses a commercial-grade 5000 psi concrete mix, the base mix will always start with gray Portland, somewhat limiting the degree of color you can achieve.

◄Basic safety equipment.

SAFETY

In general, concrete is a relatively safe material; you don't want to eat it or anything, but taking some simple precautions will keep your work with concrete enjoyable.

1 WEAR GLOVES WHEN HANDLING CONCRETE. Ideally, you should avoid direct skin contact with concrete for prolonged periods of time. Reactions from direct contact with concrete can range from slight irritations or rashes to chemical burns or allergic reactions. Wear rubber gloves and wash off any concrete that may get on your skin.

2 WEAR A DUST MASK WHEN YOU'RE MIXING CONCRETE. The dust from concrete can irritate your throat and lungs, and long-term exposure to concrete dust can lead to a serious lung condition called silicosis. Wearing a dust mask is an easy preventative measure; we use disposable dust masks with small elastic bands.

3 WEAR EYE PROTECTION if you're working on a project and concrete is flying off. We rarely get concrete in our eyes unless we are cutting or grinding it. But it is conceivable that you could splash it or rub it into your eyes, which could result in simple redness to serious chemical burns. If concrete gets into your eyes, rinse them thoroughly.

MIXING CONCRETE

There are many ways to mix concrete. The projects that follow call for mixing by hand using a margin trowel and mixing tray (for smaller projects), or with a hoe and wheelbarrow (for larger projects), or with an electric paddle mixer and bucket (also for larger projects), and also with a gas-driven drum mixer (for very large projects). The concrete for every project in this book can be mixed using a simple hoe and a mixing tray or wheelbarrow, but if you have access to a motorized tool, then mixing the concrete for

| 1. Wheelbarrow | 3. Hoe | 5. Clean bucket | 7. Electric paddle mixer |
| 2. Shovel | 4. Drill with mixing paddle | 6. Mixing tray | 8. Margin trowel |

▲ Some of the many tools used to mix concrete.

the larger projects, like the side table and oval planter, will be less tiring. Always mix the concrete thoroughly, especially if you're mixing by hand.

As a rule of thumb, the less water you add to the mix, the stronger the concrete will be. Water makes concrete workable, so it is important to have an adequate amount, but resist the temptation to keep adding water unless you really need it. You can always add more water if you need to, but you can't remove it. With a few exceptions, most of the projects in this book direct you to follow the instructions for adding water on the packaging of the mix.

FORMS AND MOLDS

Forms and molds hold the mixed concrete when it is in its liquid state until it is fully cured, giving the concrete its final shape. Form and mold are often used interchangeably, but one typical distinction is that forms are built for single-use purposes while molds are built for using multiple times. Molds are often made from rubber, plastic, and fiberglass. The projects in this book call for building forms, since we have no intention of producing multiples and our building techniques do not lend themselves to multiple castings.

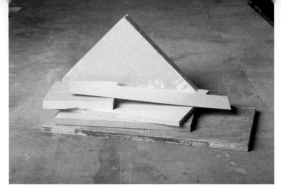

▲ From top to bottom, polystyrene foam (purple and blue), laminate, melamine, and plywood are common materials for building forms.

We use a variety of common materials to build forms. Melamine is the standard go-to choice for building forms. The melamine we use is ¾-inch particleboard that is laminated with a paper-resin coating on both sides. It's an ideal material for forms because the laminated coating is smooth and waterproof, which gives the concrete a wonderfully smooth finish. Melamine is available at home-improvement stores. Plywood is equally good, but for the very opposite reason: it gives the concrete a rough, wood-grain texture. But we are also opportunistic and will use any material we think we can make work, such as plastic trash cans, planters from nurseries, and even a plastic container that we salvaged from a recycling bin. We encourage you to use whatever material you can find for a form. Keep in mind that you have to take apart or even destroy a form when you're demolding the concrete, so don't use materials or a container that has sentimental or financial value. Once you get started building forms and your imagination takes over, you'll soon find form material everywhere, giving you the ability to turn trash into treasure.

Another invaluable material used in forms and molds is polystyrene foam. We use it to make knockouts, which take up space in the form and are useful for creating decorative inset details, for functional details, or just for reducing the volume of concrete needed to fill a form. Knockouts are embedded in the cured concrete and sometimes need to be dug out from the concrete, so if you're substituting something else for a foam knockout, don't use wood, plastic, rubber, or any material that is difficult to break up and that therefore would be nearly impossible to remove.

One last detail concerning building forms: when there's enough space to reach into a form, we always try to seal the seams of the form using silicone caulk and a caulking gun. Silicone works really well for this purpose, providing additional protection from springing a leak in the form, keeping the concrete where it belongs. It also helps retain moisture in the concrete while it's curing, resulting in a stronger, denser, and more reliable product. Silicone caulk and caulking guns can be found at any hardware or home-improvement store.

CASTING TECHNIQUES

Casting is the act of pouring, packing, or otherwise filling a form or mold with concrete. There are many ways to cast concrete, each with its own particular strengths and

▲ Pouring concrete into a form.

▲ Pressing concrete into a form by hand.

weaknesses. The design of a project often determines the appropriate casting technique, and in turn the casting technique determines the appropriate concrete mix for a project. For example, if a project is cast by hand, as the stool project is, the consistency of the concrete needs to be stiff so that it can be cast up a vertical surface without falling down the form. The projects in this book use two fundamental yet versatile casting techniques: pouring and pressing.

▲ This garden stool features the veins and bugholes that are characteristic of casting concrete using the pressing technique.

Pouring

Pouring is the technique that typically comes to mind with regard to working with concrete. Projects that are poured require tightly constructed forms that can withstand the weight of the mix and hold the liquid without springing a leak, and the concrete is mixed to a consistency that will flow from a container into a form or mold. More often than not, we pour concrete into a form that is built upside down and then demolded (the form is removed). The piece is then turned right-side up. Occasionally we build a form right-side up and, after pouring the concrete, we finish the surface using a trowel. Troweling the surface involves leveling the concrete with a screed board, and then working the concrete with a trowel to get a smooth finish.

Pressing

Pressing requires a more specialized cement mix that uses less water than mixes for other techniques. Because the mix is drier, it holds its shape more readily and can be applied to a form one handful at a time. This technique, used to cast pieces that are strong and light, results in a variety of textures, such as veins and bugholes, on the surface of the concrete. Pieces that are pressed often require two coats, a face coat and a backer coat.

Clean-up

Cleaning up after working with concrete consists of rinsing off all the tools and equipment with a garden hose and scrubbing the tougher stuff off with a brush or cloth. Never rinse or pour diluted concrete down a drain or sewer—it will continue to cure and permanently clog the pipe. If you are rinsing tools and equipment in a yard or on a lawn, be sure to dilute the concrete with enough water for it to soak into the ground. Clean your tools and equipment as soon as you've finished casting—if you let the concrete start to cure at all, cleaning up becomes exponentially more difficult.

Sealing Concrete

Sealing concrete is optional. We recommend using a sealer, but because sealers can be complicated and vary greatly in application we consider them to be outside the scope of this book. Not only do sealers protect concrete from stains, from the effects of weather, and from cracking during freeze-thaw cycles, they often make colors richer and more vibrant. Sealing concrete is not difficult. We encourage you to find out what is available in your area and follow the instructions on the manufacturer's label. Sealers are typically located in the same area as concrete in hardware and home-improvement stores.

COMMON TOOLS

There are a number of tools that you should always have on hand when you're working with concrete. The projects in this book require different tools depending on the technique used, but the tools on the opposite page will always be useful. A margin trowel is indispensable. If you work with concrete long enough you will realize the indispensability and versatility of this little tool.

COLORING CONCRETE

Coloring concrete is an exciting way to bring variety and interest to your pieces. Most concrete mixes available are made using gray Portland cement, which yields the gray we typically associate with concrete. If you intend to use darker and earth-tone colors in a project, using gray concrete is fine, but for more vibrant colors, or for when you want more control over the color, use white Portland cement. Though white Portland mixes are not as widely available as gray concrete

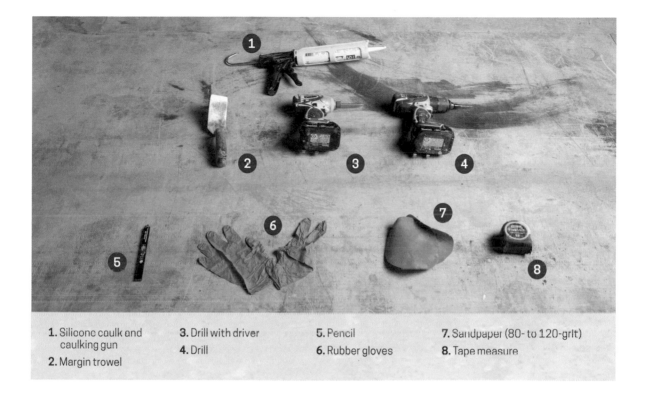

1. Silicone caulk and caulking gun
2. Margin trowel
3. Drill with driver
4. Drill
5. Pencil
6. Rubber gloves
7. Sandpaper (80- to 120-grit)
8. Tape measure

mixes, the Internet puts them within easy reach. The concrete mix you choose will determine the density, quality, and brightness of the color you can achieve. Before you begin a project, you should have an idea of what color you want to use, because the concrete you use will affect the final color.

Integral Color

Integral color describes a concrete piece that has color throughout, not just on its surface. Integral color is an easy and convenient technique to use. Because the color saturates the entire piece, if the piece is chipped the underlying concrete exposed by the chip will be the same color as the surface. Pigment used for integral color comes in dry and liquid forms. In terms of performance, there is very little difference between the two; we generally prefer dry pigment because it stores well and is easier to use. With a few exceptions, pigments are typically added toward the end of the mixing process—this allows all the other ingredients in the mix to be thoroughly combined before the color is added. Be sure to mix well after adding the pigment; otherwise the concrete may have streaks or inconsistent coloring in the final piece. Pigments used to color cement are very potent, so be sure to wear gloves when you're using pigments.

▲ Pigments for concrete come in many hues.

Color Stains

Staining is another means of applying color to concrete. Concrete floors and decorative walls are often stained with color. Unlike integral color, pigmented stains are applied after the piece has been cast, demolded, and processed (sanded and cleaned). While adding integral color to a mix results in a uniform and solid color, stains supply a more unpredictable and variegated color finish, or mottling effect. Stains are easy to apply and color only the immediate surface of the concrete and are similar to staining wood; they are not meant to disguise the natural beauty of the concrete but to enhance the texture and character. However, if a stained piece is ever chipped, the original color of concrete will show through and can be difficult to repair. We use two types of stains in this book: acid stain and water-based stains.

Acid stains do not use pigments but rather rely on a chemical reaction with the calcium hydroxide in the concrete to produce permanent, translucent, rich mottled colors. Acid stains provide a very durable and natural-looking finish. Most acid stains are a mixture of water, hydrochloric acid, and acid-soluble metallic salts. The acid in the stain penetrates and lightly etches the surface, allowing the metallic salts to work their magic and create the subtle hue changes. Because of the chemical reaction taking place, there's no control over the final look of the color. Acid staining can feel like a

► Applying slurry to a cast concrete piece.

gamble—you have to embrace a level of serendipity, but that's part of the fun. Most acid stain colors are natural earth-tone shades.

Water-based stains differ from acid stains in that they achieve color with micro-pigment particles that penetrate into the pores of the concrete. Most water-based stains are a combination of acrylic polymers and pigments. There is usually a better selection of colors available since color is achieved with pigments instead of a chemical reaction. With water-based stains, you have more control over the final look and application of color. You can layer the color and apply multiple coats if desired, and the stain remains translucent, ensuring that the texture of the concrete remains visible.

Slurry

Slurry is a loose, cement-based mix that is forced into cracks and cavities using your hands or a sponge. Slurry is used to fill voids, pinholes, or veins in cured concrete, and slurrying is the action of applying slurry. Slurry can be used to hide voids in the concrete and make them blend in with the piece or to make them stand out. Voids are often filled with the same color as used in the cast concrete, but slurrying voids is a great opportunity to add some contrast and drama to a piece by using a color that is unexpected and different. Because slurry is often applied in several coats, you can use different colors for each coat, adding texture and depth to the surface. With some casting techniques, air pockets and veins are unavoidable and even desirable. Slurry gives you an opportunity to capitalize on these imperfections and highlight them. One casting technique in particular that uses slurry extensively is the pressed technique.

A FEW WORDS ABOUT COLOR

Color may be one of the most intimidating and confusing aspects of design. A basic understanding of color opens up a world of possibility, so here is a brief introduction to basic color principles to help you make confident choices for your color concrete projects.

The best place to start exploring color is with a color wheel. A basic color wheel is composed of six colors: three primary colors—red, blue, and yellow—and three secondary colors—green, purple and orange. All colors are composed of different combinations of primary colors plus black and white. When you mix two primary colors equally, you get the secondary colors. When you mix any two primary and secondary colors equally you get tertiary colors. These are yellow-orange, red-orange, red-purple, blue-purple, blue-green, and yellow-green. Mixing can continue ad infinitum, of course, but a basic color wheel is a good place to start understanding how colors are made and how they interact.

Colors are relative to their immediate surroundings and lighting—a color appears different outdoors than it does indoors, for example, because of the quality of light.

There's a complex dynamic between color and light that can be quite surprising. This is the fun part: when colors are used together in close proximity they can affect how they each look. Sometimes this effect is dramatic.

Returning to the color wheel, colors that are directly across from one another are complementary pairs. When you mix complementary pairs you get muddy, unappealing, nondescript colors, but if you place them next to each other they make each other pop. Using complementary colors next to each other is an easy way to bring drama to a space, but the effect can also become too intense. You can mitigate the drama by reducing one color either by size or purity of hue.

Monochromatic color schemes use different values, tints, and shades of the same hue. Working with a monochromatic palette can create harmonious spaces with an elevated sense of refinement. Many people are afraid that this will yield boring results, but it can really pull a space together with a quiet strength.

Analogous color schemes make use of colors that are next to each other on the color wheel. Using an analogous color palette maintains a visual unity while still allowing for variety. These color schemes often have a calming effect on a space.

Last, we have the triadic color scheme, created when you use three colors that

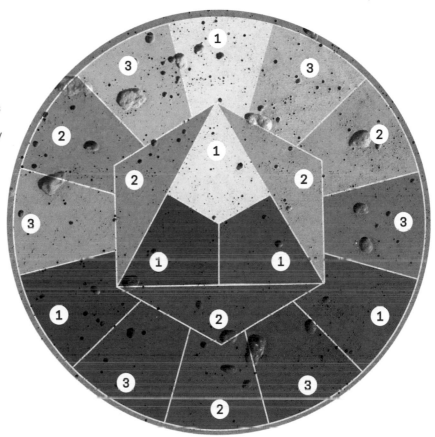

▶ The color wheel illustrates the basic relationships of colors to each other: primary (**1**), secondary (**2**), and tertiary (**3**).

are evenly spaced around the color wheel. The advantage of a triadic color scheme is that it unifies like an analogous scheme but still carries a little of the punch of the complementary.

When you're considering colors for your projects, assess the environment in which the finished piece will eventually live. Do you want a punch of color or something that will blend in? Take your inspiration from your garden—what colors appear there? Considering the colors already in your landscape and creating something that responds and interacts with them will enhance your garden even further.

PROJECTS

The projects in this book have been thoughtfully orchestrated for a breadth of experience that provides you not only with an end product, but with the know-how to integrate color into concrete pieces and an understanding of color and concrete that can be applied to any idea of your own. Once you've mastered the basic skills and techniques, you'll have a creative toolbox that will give you the freedom and ability to tailor the projects to your needs or to create your own original projects.

Before you pick up a drill or mixing tray, we encourage you to read the introduction and how-to steps for the project to familiarize yourself with it first. As we touched on earlier, in many cases you can be creative with the materials needed for some of the forms—we salvaged plastic containers and cardboard tubes from recycling bins, scoured craft and hardware stores, and even put kitchen bowls to work. We hope you will enjoy the process and be pleased with the outcome of your projects, but not completely satisfied. We want you to want more and to keep growing in your creative abilities—these pages are just the beginning of your concrete journey.

◀ A modern concrete birdhouse is just one of many projects that await you.

▲ A modern, sophisticated tabletop planter.

TABLETOP PLANTER
INTEGRAL COLOR WITH ACID STAIN

When we first made this elegant tabletop planter we were surprised by how such a simple idea could bring such sophistication, texture, and soul to its setting—it is really a testament to how small details can bring life to our surroundings. The planter holds a single plant and makes a lovely centerpiece, especially for a party or special occasion. We often use moss or stonecrop for our tabletop planters because we like their minimalist aesthetic and the layering of textures, but almost any plant will work as long as it has sufficient room for growth.

The planter measures 12 × 4 × 4 inches but can be made in any size you like. It was cast by pouring concrete into a melamine form, and color was added by spraying the planter with an acid stain to draw out the color of the natural gray concrete. Melamine is straightforward to work with, making it good form material for a beginner, and it gives concrete a smooth surface.

▼ Some of the materials needed for this project.

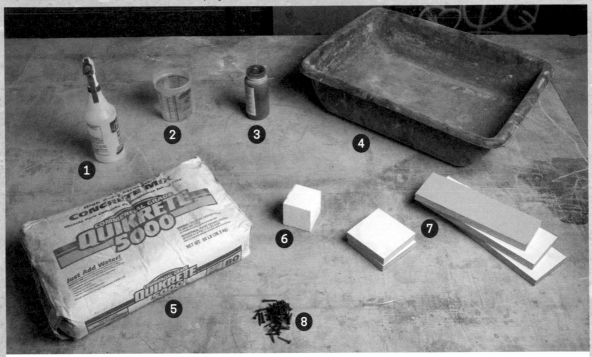

1. Clean spray bottle
2. Water
3. Acid stain
4. Mixing tray
5. Quikrete 5000 Concrete Mix
6. Polystyrene foam
7. Melamine
8. Screws

MATERIALS

- ¾-inch melamine:

  One 4 × 12-inch piece (for the base)

  Two 4¾ × 4¾-inch pieces (for the short sides)

  Two 4¾ × 12¾-inch pieces (for the long sides)

- 1¼- or 1½-inch screws
- One piece of 3 × 3 × 3-inch polystyrene foam
- Silicone caulk
- Approximately ¼ of an 80-lb. bag of Quikrete 5000 Concrete Mix
- Water
- 2-inch length of ¼-inch rubber tubing
- Plastic sheet
- Acid stain (we used a color called weathered wheat)
- Rubber gloves

TOOLS

- Table saw or circular saw
- Drill or screw gun and bit
- 5-gallon mixing tray or bucket
- Margin trowel
- Reciprocating saw (without the blade), palm sander, or hammer (for vibrating the form)
- Spray bottle
- 80- to 120-grit sandpaper
- Clean cloth or rag
- Soft brush or sponge

1 BUILD THE FORM. Begin building the melamine form by screwing the side pieces to the base and to each other. When you're using melamine, it's important to predrill the holes before you drive in the screws to prevent the melamine from splitting. Predrilling also ensures a tightly constructed form that is less likely to leak. Once the form is built, secure the foam knockout in place with silicone. We positioned the knockout at one end of the planter to give it a bit of asymmetry, but you can place it anywhere in the form as long as it doesn't touch the sides. Position the knockout so that there's a ½-inch space between it and the sides of the form.

2 MIX THE CONCRETE. Pour the cement into the mixing tray and add water as directed on the Quikrete 5000 package. The less water you use, the stronger the concrete will be, but make sure you use enough to make the mix workable. For this project, the concrete needs to flow out of the container and into the form—it should be the same consistency as really thick waffle batter. Use a margin trowel to mix the water and concrete by hand. This is a simple way to get the job done, but if you have a power mixer, feel free to use that instead.

▼ Building the form.

▼ Placing the foam knockout.

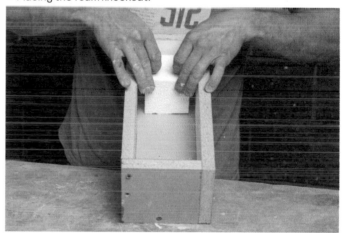

▼ Mixing by hand.

▼ Using the trowel to pack the concrete into the form.

▼ Vibrating the form to consolidate the concrete.

▼ Smoothing the top of the concrete with a margin trowel.

3 **CAST AND VIBRATE THE CONCRETE.** Once the concrete is thoroughly mixed, pour it into the form until it's level with the top edges of the form. Next, vibrate the concrete. Place a palm sander (or reciprocating saw) firmly against the side of the form, turn it on, and allow it to vibrate the form. Vibrating the concrete eliminates any air bubbles trapped in it, resulting in a much tighter, consolidated mix (the mix will be denser and have a much more consistent surface texture). After you've vibrated the concrete, use a margin trowel to level the surface of the concrete. Then insert the rubber tube into the concrete until one end makes contact with the foam knockout—the tube creates a drain hole for the planter.

4 **COVER THE FORM** loosely with plastic and let it sit overnight on a flat surface to cure.

▶ The rubber tube creates drainage for the planter.

5 **REMOVE THE FORM.** To separate the form from the cured concrete, remove the screws and gently pry off the melamine pieces. In concrete terms, gently can be misleading. Sometimes it takes a fair amount of negotiation and even brute strength to separate the form from the concrete. Be mindful that the concrete will still be fairly green—a bit soft—at this point and susceptible to damage. You can opt to wait a few days before demolding, which will give the concrete more time to harden.

6 **DIG OUT THE KNOCKOUT.** Once the planter is demolded, carefully dig out the foam knockout—a margin trowel or other flat tool can assist nicely with this process. Lacquer thinner or another type of solvent can be used to dissolve the foam if needed, but we suggest using thinner only after the majority of the foam has been removed manually.

▼ Carefully removing the sides of our form.

▼ Removing the foam knockout.

▲ Smoothing down the edges and rough spots.

7 **PROCESS.** Sand any rough edges on the planter with 80- to 120-grit sandpaper, and wipe the planter with a clean cloth to remove any dust.

8 **APPLY THE ACID STAIN.** Be sure to wear rubber gloves when you're applying acid stain, because the stain can cause your skin to dry and crack. Also, protect your work surface from the acid stain by placing the planter (supported on a few blocks of scrap wood) in a mixing tray or on a sheet of plastic. Pour the stain into a clean spray bottle and soak the entire planter with a fine mist of spray. Don't worry if the stain runs and puddles—this will add character to the finish. Let the planter dry completely before washing the residue off with water and a soft brush or sponge.

▼ Ready for staining.

▼ Saturating the surface.

▲ Concrete spheres add a colorful surprise to the garden.

CONCRETE SPHERE
INTEGRAL COLOR WITH CONTRASTING SLURRY

Spheres are simple, elegant, and beautiful objects. This project in particular is rife with possibilities because the sphere is hollow and wholly customizable by you—it can be a planter, a garden accent, even a table decoration.

One of our favorite ways to use spheres is to scatter them throughout our landscaping—they are like little gems peeking out from in between the plants. Once you've learned how to make one, you can use larger and smaller forms to make spheres in a range of sizes.

This sphere is approximately 8 inches in diameter. The form for this project is a glass light globe (for a light fixture) that we found at a local hardware store. When you're looking for a light globe for this project, make sure you can easily fit a hand through the opening—you'll be pressing the concrete by hand and will need to reach into the sphere. Pressing concrete by hand results in voids and veins in the surface of the concrete—these are desirable and perfect to highlight with a colorful slurry. We used a blue pigment for the slurry—we like the bright vibrant blue against the soft white cement.

We used Buddy Rhodes Bone White Concrete Counter Mix because it works beautifully for this pressed technique and has a claylike consistency. The raw ingredients in the mix make a really strong concrete, and all we have to do is add water. The slurry is made with high-quality white Portland cement, which allows us to achieve vibrant and contrasting colors for this project.

▼ Some of the materials needed for this project.

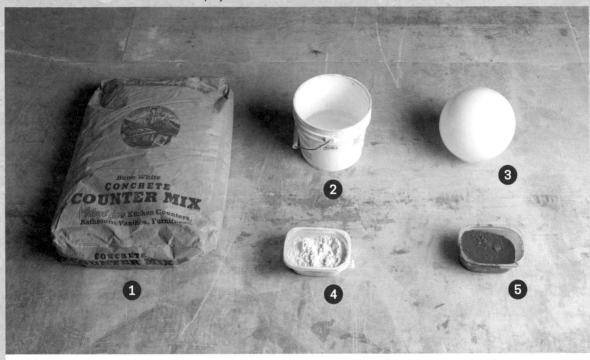

1. Buddy Rhodes Bone White
Concrete Counter Mix
2. Water

3. Globe for light fixture
4. White Portland cement

5. Pigment

MATERIALS

- One glass globe, with an 8-inch diameter, and with an opening large enough to fit a hand through
- Rubber gloves
- Approximately ⅛ of a 70-lb. bag of Buddy Rhodes Bone White Concrete Counter Mix
- Water
- Plastic sheet
- White Portland cement
- Pigment (we used a color called ultra-blue)

TOOLS

- Mixing tray or bucket
- Mixing paddle
- Hammer
- Work gloves
- Safety glasses
- Sandpaper (80- to 120-grit)
- Dust rag
- Apron (optional)
- Small bucket or plastic container
- Margin trowel
- Cheesecloth or pantyhose (optional)
- Sponge
- Bucket

1 **MIX THE CONCRETE.** Mix the concrete in a bucket or mixing tray according to the manufacturer's directions. You'll be applying the concrete to the form by hand, so the consistency of the mix needs to be thick and sticky. The amount of water it takes to reach this consistency varies (even weather conditions can affect it), so add water slowly until the mix can hold its shape and has a claylike consistency.

▼ The mix can hold its shape but is still slightly crumbly.

2 **CAST THE CONCRETE.** Be extra careful throughout this step and the following steps since the form is made of glass. Wearing gloves and using your hands, take small handfuls of concrete and press them against the inside of the glass globe, making a layer about ¾-inch thick. Start on the bottom and work your way around and up the sides of the globe. Press the sections of concrete together for strength, but keep in mind that the less you press, the more voids and veining the finished piece will have. When you reach the lip of the globe, round the concrete just over the edge where the lip begins (but not up the lip).

▼ Beginning to press the concrete into the form.

▼ A few handfuls of mix pressed in the form.

▼ The finished lip.

3 **COVER THE FORM** loosely with plastic and let it sit overnight on a flat surface to cure.

4 **REMOVE THE FORM.** First, set the sphere in a mixing tray to catch the glass as you break it. Using a hammer, gently tap on the globe to break the glass, being careful not to tap so hard that you damage or break the concrete. Be sure to wear gloves and safety glasses while you're doing this, because pieces of glass may fly off as they break. Work your way around the sphere, softly tapping until the glass falls away like a shell.

5 **PROCESS.** Lightly sand the lip to give it a more finished edge, breaking off and smoothing any sharp edges. Dust off the sphere with a dry rag.

▼ We used a plastic mixing tray to contain the broken glass.

▼ The pits and voids, which are the result of pressing the concrete by hand, are desirable.

6 MIX THE SLURRY. Pigments used to color cement are very potent, so be sure to wear rubber gloves. (Wearing an apron is a good idea, too.) To make the slurry, mix about one cup of the white Portland cement with the pigment in a small bucket or plastic container using a margin trowel and add water little by little until the slurry achieves a yogurt-like consistency. The amount of pigment you use in your mix is completely up to you—start by adding a little bit and add more until you reach a color you like. Keep in mind that the color of the wet mix will be a little darker than on the cured concrete.

If you don't want to purchase a bag of white Portland cement just for the slurry, use a cheesecloth or nylon fabric like pantyhose to strain the larger aggregates out of the Buddy Rhodes Bone White Concrete Counter Mix, leaving you with the cement and finer aggregates. Mix according to the directions in this step.

▼ Sanding the lip smooth.

▼ Mixing pigment and white cement.

▼ Mixing until the slurry achieves a yogurtlike consistency.

▼ Using a sponge to apply slurry.

▼ Cleaning off excess slurry.

7 **APPLY THE SLURRY.** Wearing gloves, apply the slurry to the sphere by hand or using a clean damp sponge. Cover the sphere with slurry, working it into all the veins and voids.

8 **PROCESS.** Once the sphere is covered with slurry, clean off the excess slurry using a damp sponge and a bucket of water. Timing is key here, if you wait too long it will be more difficult to get all the blue residue off the sphere. Begin this step when the slurry wipes off relatively easily but is not pulled out of the voids. You may have to test it; if the slurry comes off too easily, wait a bit longer. You may have to change the water in the bucket and wring the sponge out a few times. The goal is to clean the surface but not drag the slurry out of the voids.

9 **CURE THE SLURRY.** Let the piece sit overnight, until the slurry is hard. Sand the sphere lightly to remove any blue residue left on the surface.

▲ The finished white sphere with blue veins.

▲ This is a versatile planter—you can change the order of the rings as you like.

STACKED RING PLANTER
GRADATED INTEGRAL COLOR

This project demonstrates how to use one color pigment black—to achieve three shades that range from medium gray to solid black. The planter consists of three rings that, when stacked, highlight the contrasting shades and make a stylish planter. One aspect of this project that we really enjoy is that we can play with the order of the rings: stacking them like a tiered cake or like a funnel. We made three pieces here, but you can make as many as you like—the more pieces you cast the more fun you can have. Experiment and see what fits your fancy. The planter is perfect for cactus, bromeliads, stonecrop, or small ferns.

All the rings in this project are the same height, making the finished planter 4½ inches high, but feel free to try different heights. The diameter of the finished piece is 8 inches. The form uses cardboard and plastic rings, and a variety of items can be adapted to make the rings—browse at your local hardware store or scavenge your trash and recycling bins for items that will work.

▼ Some of the materials needed for this project.

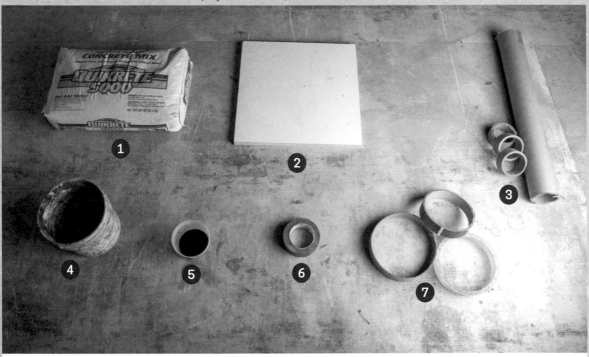

1. Quikrete 5000 Concrete Mix
2. Melamine
3. Cardboard tube (for inner form)
4. Water
5. Pigment
6. Tape
7. Rings (for the outer form)

MATERIALS

- Cardboard or plastic ring, 6 inches in diameter and 1½ inches high (for the outer ring)

- Cardboard or plastic ring, 7 inches in diameter and 1½ inches high (for the outer ring)

- Cardboard or plastic ring, 8 inches in diameter and 1½ inches high (for the outer ring)

- Three cardboard or plastic rings, 4 inches in diameter and 1½ inches high (for the inner rings)

- One 12 × 24-inch piece of 3-inch melamine (or three separate pieces that will each fit one cardboard ring, for the base)

- Silicone caulk

- Rubber gloves

- Approximately ¼ of an 80-lb. bag of Quikrete 5000 Concrete Mix

- Water

- Black pigment

- Plastic sheet

TOOLS

- Saw

- Box cutter or carpenter knife

- 80- to 120-grit sandpaper

- Painter's tape

- Caulking gun

- Bucket

- Margin trowel

1 **BUILD THE FORM.** After you cut the rings to size, clean up any burs and shavings on the edges using a knife or sandpaper. If you've used cardboard rings, tape the interior with painter's tape to cover the cardboard texture and supply a smoother finish to the concrete. Attach the outer rings to the melamine using silicone. Then set an inner ring inside each outer ring, and attach it to the melamine using silicone. We intentionally set the inner rings off center to create a more dynamic and interesting stack once the planter is finished.

2 **MIX THE CONCRETE.** Pour the cement in a bucket, add water according to the manufacturer's directions, and mix thoroughly by hand using a margin trowel until the mixture reaches a consistency that is pourable. Once you have the correct consistency, add the pigment for the first ring.

We used a black oxide pigment, but we wanted the individual rings to range in color from medium gray to black. To achieve medium gray, add a small amount of the pigment to the mixture to start. This will give you a gray that is slightly darker than unpigmented concrete. Pour the first ring (we poured the largest ring first, because we wanted it to be medium gray). Then add a little more pigment to the mixture to get a darker gray, but not black. Pour the second ring. And for the final ring, add enough

▼ Attaching the forms to the melamine.

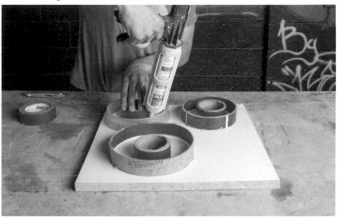

▼ The inner rings are positioned off center so that the finished stack will be asymmetric.

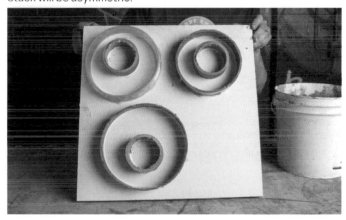

▼ Filling the forms with concrete.

▼ Shaking the melamine to vibrate the forms.

▼ Cut the forms and pull them away from the rings.

▼ Sand the rings lightly to remove any sharp edges.

pigment to turn the mix a true black. This is a simple way to use one pigment and one batch of mix and achieve three distinct shades.

We chose to make the largest ring the lightest color and the smallest ring black because the visual weight of black is much heavier than the lighter gray, so we wanted the black ring to be at the top of the planter, keeping the visual weight of the rings in proportion.

3 CAST THE CONCRETE. The concrete will level itself, so be sure to set the melamine base on a level surface—if the rings are cast on a slope they won't be flat. After you've added the first bit of pigment to the mix, pour the mix into a form, trying to be as neat as possible. Repeat with the next two shades of color and forms. Vibrate the forms once they are filled by shaking the melamine gently. Vibrating the forms helps to level and consolidate the mix. Then, level the concrete with a trowel so that it is even with the top edges of the forms.

► A lovely finished ring.

4 **COVER THE FORMS** loosely with plastic and let them sit overnight on a flat surface to cure.

5 **DEMOLD AND PROCESS.** Carefully use a sharp knife to cut off the forms—they may not slide off easily. Cut carefully so that you don't damage the concrete—it is still green at this point and scratches easily. Peel the painter's tape off the concrete. Lightly sand the rings to remove any sharp edges and to give them a more finished look by rounding the corners a bit.

▼ The stacked rings, arranged lightest to darkest, ready for a plant.

▼ Another option for stacking, smallest on the bottom to largest.

▲ Cracks and chips add to the character of the piece.

ADDRESS SIGN
INTEGRAL COLOR WITH RECESSED DESIGN

A striking addition to your home, this concrete address sign supplies handcrafted curb appeal. This project demonstrates how to use pigment to color the mix for the sign and how to capitalize on unusual finds by using them as knockouts. We used cardboard numbers that we found at a local craft store, but we've also seen foam, plastic, and metal versions. (If you use metal numbers, there is a good chance they will stay embedded in the concrete; they'll be very difficult to dig out.)

The finished address sign measures 32 × 6 × 3 inches. The Quikrete 5000 Concrete Mix lends a rough, industrial character to the project, so expect to see some cracks and chips in the finished piece. They should be embraced—cracks and chips are part of the serendipity of concrete.

▼ Some of the materials needed for this project.

1. Melamine **3.** Screws **5.** Pigment
2. Quikrete 5000 Concrete Mix **4.** Cardboard numbers

MATERIALS

- ¾-inch melamine:

    One 6 × 32-inch piece (for the base)

    Two 3¾ × 32-inch pieces (for the long sides)

    Two 3¾ × 7½-inch pieces (for the short sides)

- 1¼- or 1½-inch screws
- Silicone caulk
- Cardboard numbers
- Rubber gloves
- Approximately ¼ of an 80-lb. bag of Quikrete 5000 Concrete Mix
- Water
- Plastic sheet
- Pigment (we used red oxide, yellow shade)

TOOLS

- Table saw or circular saw
- Power drill or driver
- Caulking gun
- Mixing tray
- Margin trowel
- Small bucket or plastic container

1 **BUILD THE FORM.** Attach the long and short sides of the form to the base, remembering to predrill the holes for the screws. Apply silicone to the seams on the interior of the form to help prevent leakage.

2 **ATTACH THE NUMBER FORMS.** Keep in mind that we're working on the form from the back side, and that once the piece is finished it will be turned over. In order for the address to read properly once the piece is finished, the numbers need to be placed backward and from right to left. (Trust us, it is a terrible experience to finally see the finished work and find that a digit is reversed or the whole address is backward.) The street address for this project is 6425, but because the piece is being made from the back side, the numbers in the form read 5-2-4-6 from left to right.

Center the number forms in the melamine form, using a tape measure to make sure they're centered between the top and bottom sides and between the left and right sides. Because the numbers are different shapes, eyeball and adjust them until you're sure the spaces between them are even. Adhere them to the base with silicone, and let the silicone dry for 30 to 45 minutes.

▼ Screwing together the form.

▼ Measuring to make sure the numbers are centered in the melamine form.

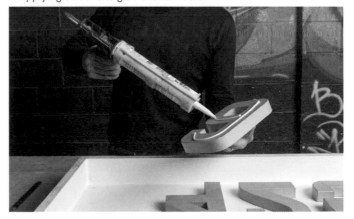
▼ Applying silicone to glue the numbers.

▼ Mixing the concrete by hand.

▼ Making sure the numbers are completely surrounded.

▼ Smoothing out the back with a margin trowel.

3 MIX THE CONCRETE. Pour the concrete into a mixing tray and add water according to the manufacturer's directions. Mix thoroughly. The consistency should be loose so that the concrete flows freely from the bucket and settles into all the nooks and crannies of the number forms. Add the pigment a little at a time until you're happy with the color, keeping in mind that the concrete will cure a bit lighter than the color of the wet mix. Fill the form to the top edge and smooth the concrete with a trowel. (The back side may never be seen, but it doesn't hurt to dress it a little.)

4 COVER THE FORM loosely with plastic and let it sit overnight on a flat surface to cure.

5 **DEMOLD AND PROCESS.** Remove the screws from the form and carefully pull off the melamine. Because the number forms are made of cardboard the moisture in the concrete makes them very easy to remove—we just used our fingers. Lightly sand down the edges of the piece.

▼ The melamine has been removed; the knockouts will be removed next.

▼ Removing the cardboard knockouts.

▼ The finished piece with inset numbers.

▲ A rustic centerpiece for candlelit dinners.

TABLETOP CANDLEHOLDER
INTEGRAL COLOR WITH OLD WORLD TEXTURE

This candleholder was inspired by the color and texture of aged, well-worn rock. Reminiscent of limestone, the candleholder's texture and timeworn character were created by coating the form with sawdust before casting the concrete.

The finished piece measures $32 \times 6\frac{3}{4} \times 3$ and fits eight small candles. To make the holes for the candles, we used round cardboard containers for knockouts (we found them at a local craft shop). If you opt to use a different type of knockout, be sure it can be easily removed after casting.

▼ Some of the materials needed for this project.

1. Quikrete 5000 Concrete Mix
2. Water
3. Spray contact adhesive
4. Melamine
5. Pigment
6. Rubber gloves
7. Round cardboard containers
8. Sawdust
9. Screws

MATERIALS

- Approximately ⅓ of an 80-lb. bag of Quikrete 5000 Concrete Mix
- Pigment (we used brown)
- ¾-inch medium-density fiberboard (MDF):
    One 6 × 32-inch piece (for the base)
    Two 3¾ × 32-inch pieces (for the long sides)
    Two 3¾ × 7½-inch pieces (for the short sides)
- Spray contact adhesive (we like Super 77)
- 1 to 2 cups of sawdust
- Rubber gloves
- Spacer blocks (ours measured 1½ inches wide)
- Eight round cardboard containers, about 2 inches in diameter
- 1¼- to 1½-inch screws

TOOLS

- Drill or screw gun
- Small drill bit
- Tape measure
- Pencil
- Hot glue gun
- Mixing tray or bucket
- Margin trowel
- Small plastic container
- Table saw or circular saw
- Propane torch (oh yeah, this is going to be fun!)
- Stiff-bristled brush

1 BUILD THE FORM. Screw the side pieces of the form to the base and to each other, predrilling the holes with a small drill bit first. Measure and mark the position of the knockouts in the center of the form. Using hot glue or silicone, attach the knockouts to the form, open side down, 1½ inches apart. Use a 1½-inch-wide spacer block or a tape measure to ensure that the space between the knockouts is even.

2 ADD TEXTURE TO THE FORM. Once the cardboard knockouts are set, cover the form with an uneven and gloopy coat of spray adhesive. Sprinkle sawdust on the form. Be generous—the more sawdust you can get to stick, the more texture you will have in the end. You may even want to repeat the spray-and-sprinkle process a couple of times to get really good texture.

▼ Screwing the end pieces to the form.

▼ Adhering the knockouts to the form with hot glue.

▼ Using a spacer block to make sure the spaces between knockouts are even.

▼ Applying a heavy coat of adhesive.

▼ Covering the coated form with sawdust.

▼ Hand mixing with pigment and water.

3 **MIX THE CONCRETE.** Pour the concrete mix into a mixing tray and add water according to the manufacturer's directions. Mix well. Add the pigment, and mix it in thoroughly. The mix should have a consistency that flows but doesn't splash—it should resemble thick waffle batter.

4 **CAST THE CONCRETE.** Using a small plastic container, carefully pour the mix into the form. There is no need to vibrate; just fill the form with concrete until it is level with the top edge of the form. Using a margin trowel, smooth out the top of the concrete.

▼ Pouring the mix carefully into the form.

5 **COVER THE FORM** loosely with plastic and let it sit overnight on a flat surface to cure.

6 **DEMOLD AND PROCESS.** Remove the screws and use a margin trowel to pry off the form. You should see lots of holes and voids filled with sawdust. Use a stiff-bristled brush to remove all the loose sawdust. Use a propane torch to clean out the pieces of sawdust still embedded in the concrete. The burning sawdust helps highlight the texture of the concrete. If you want more color and highlights, just clean out less sawdust with the brush.

▼ The form, filled to the top with concrete and ready to cure.

▼ Carefully removing the form with a margin trowel.

▼ Using the torch to burn out the sawdust.

▼ Beginning to get some coloration.

▲ Your very own ball and chain, faithfully holding the door open.

DOORSTOP
INTEGRAL COLOR WITH EMBEDDED OBJECT

Here we bring the proverbial ball and chain to life as a doorstop. It's a light-hearted conversation piece and a great example of making use of unconventional materials for a form—in this case, a child's ball. We conveniently procured a rubber ball from a playroom, but if you are not comfortable hijacking children's toys, you'll be able to find a ball at a toy store.

The color is integral—the pigment is added to the concrete mix. This project also provides an example of how to embed structural components during casting. The doorstop is 10 inches in diameter, weighs about 10 pounds, and has a 36-inch-long chain attached to it.

▼ Some of the materials needed for this project.

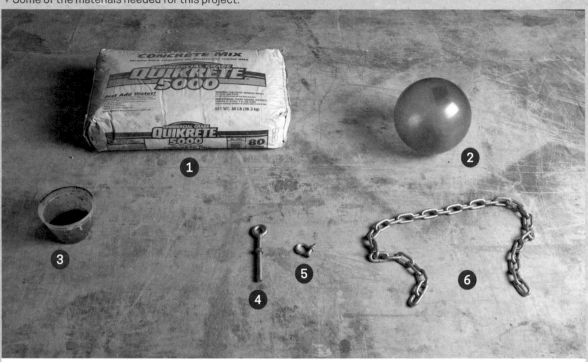

1. Quikrete 5000 Concrete Mix
2. Rubber ball
3. Pigment
4. Eye bolt
5. Screw gate shackle
6. Chain

MATERIALS

- 10-inch rubber ball
- Approximately ¼ of an 80-lb. bag of Quikrete 5000 Concrete Mix
- Water
- Pigment (we used black oxide)
- 3- to 6-inch eye bolt
- Nut (one that fits the eye bolt)
- Screw gate shackle (the shackle must fit through the eye bolt and chain)
- 36-inch length of chain

TOOLS

- Sharp scissors
- Funnel (with at least a ¾-inch opening)
- Margin trowel
- Bucket
- Towel or rag
- 18-gauge wire
- Inflation pump needle for the ball
- Bucket with a diameter that's slightly wider than the ball

1 PREPARE THE SLING AND FORM.

This project requires creating a makeshift sling to support the rubber form without deforming it. Place a towel across a small bucket and lightly press the ball into it to create a ball-shaped support. With the towel in place, wrap a length of wire around the top lip of the bucket and tighten it. The wire needs to be tight because the towel (and the wire) will support the weight of the concrete as it's cast.

Deflate the ball by inserting the pump needle into the ball to let the air out. Next, use sharp scissors to carefully cut a small hole around the area where you inserted the needle. The hole should be just big enough to insert the funnel, but small enough for the ball to retain its shape. Try to cut a very clean, round hole because straight or jagged cuts can cause the rubber to tear. (Our ball tore. The hole we cut was not as clean as it should have been, which was likely why the rubber tore. Be gentle while you're casting the concrete.)

▼ The wire secured around the towel, holding the makeshift sling together.

▼ The perfect support for the form.

▼ Deflating the rubber ball.

▼ Trying to cut a clean opening in the ball.

▼ The sort-of-round and sort-of-smooth hole that we cut. This is probably why our form tore.

▼ Adding black pigment to the mix.

2 MIX THE CONCRETE. Pour the concrete into a bucket. Add enough water and mix using a margin trowel until the concrete reaches a consistency that's pourable but still stiff enough to sit on a trowel. The concrete needs to move easily through the funnel. The consistency of the concrete is an important aspect of this project, so add the water slowly while you're mixing. (Remember, you can always add more water, but you can't take it out.) When you achieve the right consistency, add the pigment little by little until the concrete is the color you want, keeping in mind that the color of the finished piece will be a bit lighter than the color of the wet concrete. We kept adding black oxide pigment until we had a very dark black.

3 CAST THE CONCRETE. Place the ball into the towel sling and begin filling it with concrete through the funnel or by hand. Be patient and gentle with the form—the last thing you want to happen now is for it to tear, spilling all the concrete. As the form is filled, the concrete should naturally take the shape of the ball. To top off the form, remove the funnel and finish casting by hand, gently packing the last of the concrete. Once the form is full, attach the nut to the eye bolt and insert the eye bolt into the concrete through the hole.

▼ Mixing by hand with a margin trowel.

▼ The funnel we used was not cooperating, so we ended up packing the concrete into the ball by hand.

▼ Inserting the eye bolt into the concrete through the hole.

▼ Ready to be covered in plastic to cure overnight.

4 **COVER THE FORM** loosely with plastic and let it sit overnight on a flat surface to cure.

5 **DEMOLD.** Demolding this form is easy. Using a box cutter or scissors, cut the rubber, taking care not to cut so deeply that you scratch the fresh surface of the concrete. Once the rubber is removed, attach the chain to the eye bolt using the shackle.

▼ Tearing the form off of the cast.

▼ Attaching the chain using the shackle.

▲ Ready to be put to work.

▲ These pendants add a modern, colorful accent to the garden.

HANGING CONCRETE PENDANTS

INTEGRAL COLOR WITH TWO-TONE ACID STAIN

This trio of pendants will add flair to your garden, creating a simple but dynamic point of interest. For the color, we used white concrete and dipped the cast pendants into two different acid stains— one end into one color and the other end into another color—to get interesting textures and color variations.

These are thin pieces, measuring approximately 15 × 1 × 2 inches, so we used a higher-performance concrete mix that is light but strong and ideal for delicate projects like this one. Knockouts create a rectangular hole in each pendant to run a length of rope through.

▼ Some of the materials needed for this project.

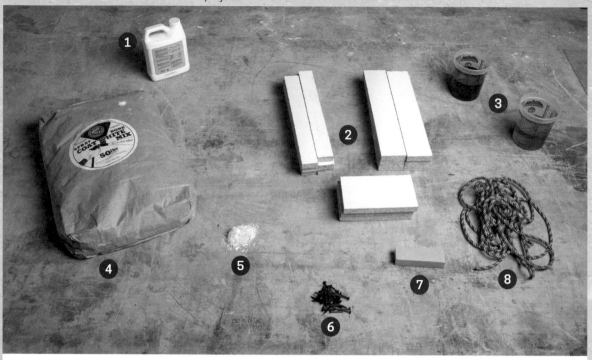

1. Water reducer
2. Melamine
3. Acid stains
4. Buddy Rhodes Bone White Spray Coat
5. PVA fibers
6. Screws
7. Polystyrene foam
8. Rope

MATERIALS

- ¾-inch melamine:

    Six 2¾ × 15-inch pieces (for the wide sides)

    Six 1¾ × 15-inch pieces (for the narrow sides)

    Three 4 × 6-inch pieces (for the bases)

- Rubber gloves
- Approximately ¼ of a 50-lb. bag of Buddy Rhodes Bone White Spray Coat
- Water
- Water reducer
- PVA fibers
- Two acid stains (we used powder blue and burnished copper)
- Three ½ × 1 × 1-inch pieces of polystyrene foam
- 1¼-inch screws
- Silicone caulk
- Plastic sheet
- 12-inch-deep plastic container
- Rope

TOOLS

- Table saw or circular saw
- Power drill or driver
- Pencil
- Caulking gun
- Bucket and drill with mixing paddle, or a trowel
- Margin trowel
- Small bucket
- Kitchen scale
- Box cutter or carpenter's knife
- Sponge

1 BUILD THE FORMS. Each form will consist of two 2¾ × 15-inch side pieces, two 1¾ × 15-inch side pieces, and one 4 × 6-inch bottom piece. The pieces for the forms are very narrow, so it is especially important to predrill the holes for the screws. See the photo (bottom right) for how to position the pieces of the form. Positioning the pieces this way helps prevent the small pieces of melamine from splitting when the screws are inserted. Screw three sides of each form together, leaving off one of the 2¾ × 15-inch side pieces. Then position one foam knockout in each form, centered on the wide side, with the ½-inch side down, about 1 inch from the top end, and adhere them to the forms using silicone. Screw on the last side of each form.

▼ Screwing a form together.

▼ The three forms, ready for the foam knockouts.

▼ The forms with the foam knockouts in place.

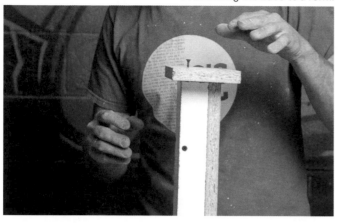

▼ Attaching the base to a form.

▼ The finished forms ready to be poured.

▼ Using a kitchen scale to measure the ingredients for the mix.

Next, place each form on a 4 × 6-inch base piece of melamine and use a pencil to outline the form on the base piece. Use the outline to guide you as you predrill the holes for the screws that will hold the base to the rest of the form. Before you drill the screws in, use silicone to adhere the base to the form to ensure a good seal. Screw the base to the form.

2 MIX THE CONCRETE. Because the pendants are so thin and delicate, they call for just a small amount of the more advanced concrete mix that we're using. This mix uses white Portland cement and contains a smaller aggregate along with other admixtures, such as pozzolans and a dry polymer, which allows us to cast really thin pieces. This project requires precise measuring, so use a kitchen scale. Carefully measure the following amounts in small containers on the kitchen scale. Pour all the ingredients into a bucket and mix until the

► Mixing the concrete with a drill and paddle.

mixture reaches the consistency of runny pancake batter. We made two batches in order to fill all three pendants; if you are going to make any alterations to the project use the same ratio of mix ingredients.

- 1600 grams of Buddy Rhodes Bone White Spray Coat
- 400 grams of water
- 8 grams of water reducer
- 2 grams of PVA fibers

3 **CAST THE CONCRETE.** Pour the mix into the forms, filling them to the top edge.

4 **COVER THE FORMS** loosely with plastic and let them sit overnight on a flat surface to cure.

▼ Pouring the forms.

▼ Filled to the top, ready to cure.

▼ Demolding a pendant.

5 **DEMOLD AND PROCESS.** Remove the screws from the form, pry off the melamine, and dig out the foam knockouts. Sand the corners and edges smooth with 80- to 120-grit sandpaper.

6 **APPLY THE ACID STAINS.** Wear rubber gloves when you're working with acid stains. When you're thinking about how high up the pendants you want the first color to reach, keep in mind that all three pendants will be soaking in a container, and the level of the stain will rise once the pendants are added to the container, causing the color to rise higher around the pendants. Pour one of the acid stains into a 12-inch-deep plastic container and soak one end of the pendants in the stain for about five minutes. Remove the pendants and set them on the lengths of wood to dry (elevating them above the

▼ Digging out a knockout with a box cutter.

▼ Smoothing the edges with sandpaper.

▼ One end of the pendants soaking in the first stain.

work surface helps protect the stain). Pour the first stain back in the original packaging to save for another use, rinse the container thoroughly, and pour the second stain into the container. Place the other end of the pendants in the second stain and let them soak for about five minutes. Remove the pendants, let them dry completely on the wood blocks, and then wash off the residue with a soft sponge and water.

7 HANG THE PENDANTS. Thread lengths of rope through the holes and hang the pendants from a tree or patio roof.

▼ Drying while we change out the stain.

▼ Staining the other end of the pendants.

▼ Allowing time for the stain to dry and chemically react with the concrete. Once the residue is rinsed off, the true color comes through.

▲ A great way to start the day.

SIMPLE DISH
INTEGRAL COLOR WITH INLAID SLURRY

Fruit, flowers, and found objects all look special displayed in this dish—it's a beautiful foundation for any centerpiece. This project demonstrates how to integrate color into the concrete body, inlay a stencil to create a pattern in the concrete, and use a contrasting color of slurry to highlight the pattern. To achieve a purple hue, we mixed red oxide and ultra-blue, and we used yellow slurry as a contrasting color.

Because this tray is about ½-inch thick at its thinnest part, it calls for a more advanced mix of concrete that remains strong even for a thin piece. The dish measures 16 × 5 × 1 inches.

▼ Some of the materials needed for this project.

1. Water reducer
2. Spray contact adhesive
3. Melamine
4. Laminate
5. Buddy Rhodes Bone White Spray Coat
6. Felt stencil
7. Pigment
8. PVA fibers
9. Water

MATERIALS

- ¾-inch melamine:

    One 16 × 5-inch piece (for the base)

    Two 1¾ × 16-inch pieces (for the long sides)

    Two 1¾ × 6½-inch pieces (for the short sides)

- 1¼- or 1½-inch screws
- One 16 × 5¼-inch piece of laminate
- Silicone caulk
- Approximately ¼ of a 50-lb. bag of Buddy Rhodes Bone White Spray Coat
- Water
- Water reducer
- PVA fibers
- Three pigments: red oxide (blue shade); ultra blue (yellow shade); yellow oxide (for the slurry)
- Felt stencil (from a local craft store)
- Spray contact adhesive (we like Super 77)
- Plastic sheet

TOOLS

- Table saw or circular saw
- Power drill or driver
- Rubber gloves
- Bucket
- Margin trowel
- Caulking gun
- Small bowl
- Kitchen scale
- Propane torch
- Small container
- Sponge
- 80- to 120-grit sandpaper

1 **BUILD THE FORM.** Using a table saw or a circular saw, cut a groove down the length of the long side of one of the 1¾ × 16-inch pieces of melamine ¾-inch from the bottom edge. Do the same on the other 1¾ × 16-inch piece of melamine. These two pieces will be opposite each other in the form, and the grooves will hold the piece of laminate in place. Once your grooves are made, attach all the sides to the 16 × 5-inch piece of melamine (the base piece), except for one short side. Remember to predrill the holes to ensure a tight seal around the form. Slide the laminate into the grooves. Because the laminate is slightly wider than the form, it will bow slightly—the bow gives the dish its concave shape. This is an easy way to introduce curves into a project. Screw the final side of the form to the base and apply silicone to the seams along the laminate and the corners of the form.

▼ The form with three sides attached—note the grooves along the sides.

▼ Sliding the laminate into the grooves.

▼ Siliconing the seams of the form.

▼ Cutting the stencil.

2 APPLY THE STENCIL. Measure and cut the stencil to the size you'd like to use, keeping in mind that you'll need a minimum border of ¼ inch between the stencil and the sides of the form to ensure that the tray has a strong edge. Once the stencil is cut to size, spray it with contact adhesive. Carefully center the stencil on the laminate, sprayed-side down, and press it against the laminate—the stencil will create the inlaid design on the tray.

▼ Spraying the stencil with contact adhesive.

▼ Carefully placing the stencil in the form.

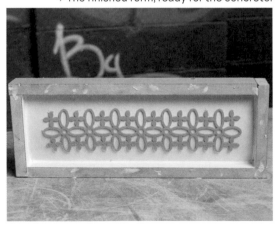

▼ The finished form, ready for the concrete.

3 **MIX THE CONCRETE.** This project requires a high strength-to-weight ratio, so we are using a more performance-oriented mix—Buddy Rhodes Bone White Spray Coat. It's critical to measure the amount of mix accurately, so use a kitchen scale to measure the ingredients. Measure the following amounts in a small container set on a kitchen scale, and pour each into a bucket for mixing:

- 1600 grams of Buddy Rhodes Bone White Spray Coat
- 400 grams of water
- 8 grams of water reducer
- 2 grams of PVA fibers
- Pigments (except for the slurry pigment)

Mix thoroughly until you have a pourable consistency that resembles pancake batter. The water reducer may take a few minutes to activate, so give it time and keep mixing until the mix is a workable consistency. Add the pigments until the concrete reaches the color you want (a small amount of pigment goes a long way, so add the pigments little by little). Pour the concrete into the form, lightly tapping it occasionally to work out any air bubbles. Smooth out the surface with a margin trowel.

▼ Adding the blue and red pigments to make purple.

▼ Cast the concrete over the stencil.

▼ The finished cast.

▼ Removing the form.

4 **COVER THE FORM** loosely with plastic and let it sit overnight on a flat surface to cure.

5 **DEMOLD.** Remove all the screws and carefully pull off the melamine and laminate.

▼ Peeling off the laminate.

▼ Cutting out the stencil.

6 REMOVE THE STENCIL. Once the form is removed from the tray, remove the stencil with a box cutter or knife. Work carefully so that you don't scratch the fresh concrete. This step can be tricky—sections of our stencil came out easily, while other parts were difficult. We resorted to carefully burning it out with a propane torch, which worked fine on the felt stencil. Depending on the stencil design and material, you may need to simply dig it out patiently using a box cutter or carpenter's knife. If small parts of the stencil remain lodged in the concrete, you can try to cover them with slurry.

7 MIX AND APPLY THE SLURRY. For the infill slurry, mix about ¼ cup of Buddy Rhodes Bone White Spray Coat with water until it reaches the consistency of thick yogurt. Once the consistency is right, add the pigment a little at a time until you are happy with the color. Apply the slurry with a trowel, making sure that all the corners and details of the stencil are filled. When the slurry begins to develop a haze, begin wiping and cleaning the residue with a wet sponge. Be careful to clean only the surface of the tray and not pull any slurry out of the pattern. If the slurry is being pulled out, wait another 10 to 15 minutes and try again.

▼ Burning out the stencil with a torch.

▼ Mixing the slurry.

▼ Pressing slurry into stencil void.

▼ Cleaning slurry with a wet sponge.

8 **FINISH.** Let the slurry cure overnight and then give the piece a light sanding all over. The sanding will clean up any slurry residue and smooth out the edges.

▼ Sanding slurry residue.

▲ The cleaned and sanded tray.

▲ The side table is perfect for a quiet morning on the porch.

SIDE TABLE
INTEGRAL COLOR WITH MULTIPLE SLURRIES

Integral color along with three colored slurries create a subtle layering of colors in this piece, giving it an understated beauty. The integral color used for the body of the table is green oxide pigment, and the slurry accent colors are gray, red, and black.

The form is made from a large plastic planter that we found at a home-improvement store; it was the perfect size for a sitting area on a porch or patio, or in a garden. The concrete is cast by hand—you'll be pressing handfuls of concrete against the side of the form, which results in voids and veins that give the piece a wonderful texture that's further enhanced by the three slurries. The table measures 36 inches in diameter and is about 18 inches high.

▼ Some of the materials needed for this project.

1. Water

2. Large plastic planter

3. Melamine

4. Clean spray bottle

5. Pigment for the concrete mix

6. Pigment for the slurry

7. Sponge

8. Buddy Rhodes Bone White Concrete Counter Mix

MATERIALS

- Plastic planter, 36 inches in diameter and about 18 inches high
- Piece of melamine that's slightly bigger than the diameter of the planter
- Silicone caulk
- Rubber gloves
- One 70-lb. bag of Buddy Rhodes Bone White Concrete Counter Mix
- Water
- White Portland cement
- Green oxide pigment
- Gray pigment
- Red oxide pigment
- Black pigment
- Plastic sheet

TOOLS

- Tape measure (or a piece of wood to use as a guide)
- Felt marker
- Box cutter or carpenter's knife
- Handsaw
- Caulking gun
- Extra-large bucket with a paddle mixer (or a wheelbarrow and hoe)
- Margin trowel
- Small container
- Spray bottle
- Sponge
- 80- to 120-grit sandpaper

1 **BUILD THE FORM.** Begin modifying the planter by carefully cutting off the bottom using a handsaw. The top of the planter will become the top of the table—cutting off the bottom gives you access to the form through the bottom. It's imperative that the bottom and top be parallel, so that the table is level, so use a tape measure or a piece of wood as a guide to mark a straight line to cut along. Then, cut off the bottom using a handsaw.

Place the planter upside down (top-side down) on the melamine and adhere it to the melamine by running silicone around the outside edge and smoothing it with your finger. Let the silicone dry for 30 minutes.

2 **MIX AND COLOR THE CONCRETE.** Pour the concrete into the bucket, add water according to the manufacturer's directions, and mix thoroughly. The consistency should be stiff enough that it holds its shape when pressed into a ball. Add the green oxide pigment and mix thoroughly.

▼ Marking the cut.

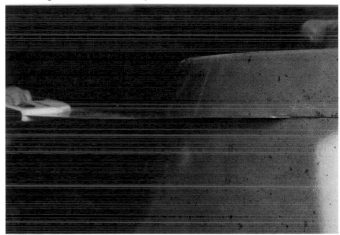
▼ Cutting the bottom of the planter off with a handsaw.

▼ Using silicone to attach the form to the melamine.

▼ We used a large bucket and electric paddle mixer to mix the concrete.

3 APPLY THE FACE COAT. There are two rounds of casting for this project—the first coat is the face coat and the second coat is the backer coat. To apply the face coat, wearing gloves, press handfuls of the mix firmly into the bottom of the form, pressing it firmly into the area where the form and melamine meet, and work out across the bottom and then up the sides of the form. Keep in mind that the less you press, the more voids and veining the finished piece will have. The face coat should be ½- to ¾-inch thick. Give the face coat some time to stiffen and set so that when you apply the backer coat the face coat won't move. The face coat should be fairly hard but still moist enough to create a good bond with the next coat of concrete. This could take 20 to 30 minutes in the summer and more than an hour in the winter.

▼ The perfect consistency.

▼ Pressing out the bottom of the form.

▼ Carefully working up the sides.

4 APPLY THE BACKER COAT. The backer coat reinforces the face coat, adding strength to the table. Before applying the backer coat, add some water to the remaining concrete mix in the bucket and mix until the concrete is smooth but still sticky enough to hang on the sides of the form without slumping. Take your time during this step so you can make sure the face coat stays intact and doesn't slump down or fall off the form. In the end, the total thickness of the two coats should be 1 to 1¼ inch. Smooth out the top lip of the concrete so that it's even with the edge of the planter.

5 COVER THE FORM loosely with plastic and let it sit overnight on a flat surface to cure.

6 DEMOLD. Separate the sheet of melamine from the form by cutting away the silicone with a box cutter. Once the melamine is detached, slice the planter with the box cutter, making a shallow cut and being careful not to damage the surface of the fresh concrete. Pull off the form.

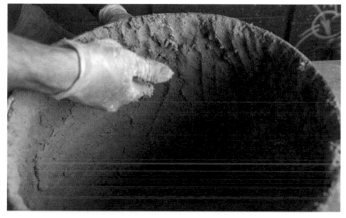
▼ Applying the backer coat.

▼ Smoothing the surface.

▼ Cutting the silicone.

▼ Cutting the mold.

▼ Pulling the form off the table.

▼ Preparing the surface for slurry.

7 MIX AND APPLY THE GRAY SLURRY.

We used three different slurries to add subtle depth and texture to the table. The mixing procedure is the same for each color. Place the pigment, along with about two cups of white Portland cement, and water, in a container and mix until the consistency is yogurt-like. Mix each slurry immediately before applying it. (Don't prepare the three slurries at the same time—each coat of slurry will need to partially cure before the next coat is applied.) Before applying each slurry, wet the surface of the concrete with either a spray bottle or sponge; otherwise the raw concrete will suck all the moisture out of the slurry and make it more difficult to apply.

Mix the gray slurry first. Wearing gloves, apply the gray slurry by hand or with a damp sponge. Skim the surface to apply a light coat all over the table, leaving some voids empty so the following coats of slurry will have voids to fill; then wipe the table clean with a damp sponge. You may need to change the water a couple of times as you are cleaning off the slurry residue. Let this coat begin to cure and dry before applying the second coat.

If you don't want to purchase a bag of white Portland cement just for the slurry, use a cheesecloth or nylon fabric like pantyhose to strain the larger aggregates out of the Buddy Rhodes Bone White Concrete Counter Mix, leaving you with the cement and finer aggregates. Mix according to the directions in this step.

8 **MIX AND APPLY THE RED OXIDE AND BLACK SLURRY COATS.** For the second coat of slurry we used red oxide. Combined with the Portland cement, it creates a nice contrast to the gray. Mix and apply the red oxide slurry following the same process described in step 7. Finally, mix and apply the coat of black slurry, following the process described in step 7. The black slurry helps calm down the red and provides more contrast. By applying multiple layers of color with this slurry technique, you get an opportunity to experiment and learn how colors react to one another.

Timing is everything when cleaning and removing the slurry residue from the concrete. If you wait too long after coating the concrete, the residue will become very difficult to remove. Begin this step when the slurry wipes off relatively easily but is not pulled out of the voids. You may have to test it; if the slurry comes off too easily, wait a bit longer.

9 **PROCESS.** Let the slurry cure for 24 hours before lightly sanding it with fine-grit sandpaper. Sanding will remove the residue and help distinguish the layers of color.

▼ Applying the coat of gray slurry.

▼ The table, covered with the gray coat of slurry.

▼ Red slurry on top of gray.

▲ The stool can also be used as a handy table while you're working in the garden.

PRESSED STOOL
INTEGRAL COLOR WITH TONE-ON-TONE SLURRY

This vibrantly colored stool features integral color and a slurry, both in the same hue. We often call this color combination tone-on-tone, and it gives a nice coherency and subtle depth to the surface. When we want the concrete for a project to be strong, bright, and pure, we use white Portland cement.

This project also explores ways we can take a simple everyday object like a plastic trash can and transform it into a form to create a good-looking and functional stool. For the form, we sourced a small plastic trash can from a local hardware store that we thought was the right size and shape for a stool. Half the fun of this project is taking a mundane object like a trash can and transforming it into something completely new and unrecognizable. We hope this will give you fresh eyes for seeing the possibilities that abound in the everyday things we come in contact with.

The concrete is cast by hand in a vertical form, which will create voids and veins that are highlighted with the slurry. The finished stool measures $12 \times 8 \times 18$ inches.

▼ Some of the materials needed for this project.

1. Plastic trash can

2. Water

3. Buddy Rhodes Bone White Concrete Counter Mix

4. Melamine

5. Silicone caulk and caulking gun

6. Pigment

7. Polystyrene foam

MATERIALS

- One nicely shaped, 18-inch-high plastic trash can
- 1 × 12 × 12-inch piece of polystyrene foam
- Silicone caulk
- 24 × 24-inch piece of ¾-inch melamine
- Approximately ½ of a 70-lb. bag of Buddy Rhodes Bone White Concrete Counter Mix
- Water
- Pigment (we used yellow)
- White Portland cement
- Plastic sheet

TOOLS

- Tape measure
- Felt marker or pencil
- Box cutter or carpenter's knife
- Caulking gun
- Mixing tray
- Mixing paddle
- Rubber gloves
- Margin trowel
- Small plastic container for mixing slurry
- Bucket
- Sponge
- 80- to 120-grit sandpaper

1 **PREPARE THE FORM.** The bottom of the trash can will become the seat (or the top) of the stool, so the first step in transforming the trash can into a form is to slice off the bottom. Turn the trash can over, measure how much of the bottom you want to cut off (the finished stool should be about 18 inches high), and use a felt marker to draw a line around the can to guide your cut. Using a box cutter or carpenter's knife, slice off the bottom of the trash can, making a clean, even cut all around.

2 **MAKE THE KNOCKOUTS.** Making the foam knockouts for the legs and feet of the stool is a great opportunity to be creative. This single step does the most to remove any evidence that a trash can was used as the form to create the stool. As you design the knockouts, keep in mind that taller knockouts will create taller legs. The shape of the knockouts should complement the finished shape of the stool. If the trash can has a rounded shape, make the knockouts rounded; if the trash can has a geometric shape, make the knockouts geometric.

The corners of the trash can will form the four legs of the stool. The space between each leg will be blocked out with the foam inside the trash can. Measure and cut the foam to the desired shape, and adhere the knockouts in place inside the trash can with silicone. Casting the concrete around the foam blocks will create the shape of the stool's legs.

▼ Marking the cut.

▼ Carefully cutting our line.

▼ Cutting the foam for the knockouts.

▼ Adhering the knockouts to the form.

3 ADHERE THE FORM TO THE MELAMINE. Set the cut end of the trash can on the melamine, and adhere it to the melamine by applying silicone around the outside edge. This will create the seat of the stool and base of the form. Let the silicone dry for 30 minutes.

▼ Attaching the form to the base with silicone.

4 MIX AND COLOR THE CONCRETE. Most of the time we use dry pigments—this project was an exception; we used a liquid pigment. Add the pigment and water to the concrete mix until the consistency resembles a crumbly clay; the concrete should hold its shape when pressed into a ball.

▼ Adding the water and pigment to the cement.

5 PRESS THE FACE COAT.

There are two rounds of casting concrete for this project—the first coat is the face coat and the second coat is the backer coat. To apply the face coat, wearing gloves, take small handfuls of concrete mix and press them into the form starting at the bottom and working up the walls of the trash can, making a layer that is ½- to ¾-inch thick. Be sure to press the concrete firmly into the corners of the base. If the trash can is especially flimsy, support the can by pressing on the outside wall with one hand as you press the concrete to the inside walls with the other. Press the concrete around the foam knockouts, not over them, pushing the concrete tightly against the sides of each knockout so that the edges of the legs will be crisp and sharp. Let the concrete set until it stiffens a bit so that when you apply the backer coat the face coat won't move. This could be anywhere from 15 minutes to an hour depending on the temperature (it may take longer if the weather is cool). The face coat should be fairly hard but still moist enough to create a good bond with the next coat of concrete.

▼ Mixing by hand with a margin trowel and mixing tray.

▼ Beginning to press out the form.

▼ Carefully pressing around our foam knockouts.

▼ Applying the backer coat.

▼ Finished casting.

▼ Sanding the feet and legs.

6 PRESS THE BACKER COAT. The backer coat reinforces the face coat, adding strength to it. Before applying the backer coat, add some water to the remaining concrete mix in the mixing tray and mix until the concrete is smooth but still sticky. Using your hands (still wearing gloves), smear handfuls of concrete onto the face coat. Give the top edge a smooth, even surface because it will be in contact with the ground once the stool is finished and turned over. The combined thickness of the two coats should be 1 to 1¼ inches.

7 COVER THE FORM loosely with plastic and let it sit overnight on a flat surface to cure.

8 DEMOLD AND PROCESS. Before removing the form, lightly sand the feet of the stool. Then, using a box cutter or carpenter's knife, cut away the silicone adhering the form to the melamine and separate the two. Dig out the foam knockouts using a margin trowel. Using a box cutter or carpenter's knife, carefully slice the form and lift it off the stool. The concrete is freshly cured and still soft at this point, so make a shallow slice to avoid cutting the concrete. Sand the exterior of the stool lightly to knock off any sharp edges.

9 **MIX THE SLURRY.** Mix the pigment and water with 2 to 3 cups of white Portland cement until it reaches a thick yogurt-like consistency. If you don't want to purchase a bag of white Portland cement just for the slurry, use cheesecloth or nylon fabric like pantyhose to strain the larger aggregates out of the Buddy Rhodes Bone White Concrete Counter Mix, leaving you with the cement and finer aggregates. Mix according to the directions in this step.

10 **APPLY THE SLURRY.** Wearing gloves, use your hands or a damp sponge to apply the slurry. We left some of the voids on the legs empty because we like the textural element that brings, but you may want to fill them completely. Either way looks terrific. Fill all the voids on the seat, however, for a more pleasant sitting experience.

▼ Carefully cutting the form.

▼ The reveal.

▼ The slurry, with its perfectly smooth yogurt-like consistency.

▼ Filling in the slurry by hand.

▼ Cleaning excess slurry with a damp sponge and water.

11 CLEAN THE SLURRY.

At this point, timing is everything; wait too long and the slurry will be difficult to remove, but clean too soon and you will pull slurry out of the voids. Begin this step when the slurry wipes off relatively easily but is not pulled out of the voids. You may have to test it; if the slurry comes off too easily, wait a bit longer.

You will need to pay close attention because not only are you working with a specific window of opportunity, but also this window can change according to weather, humidity, or materials used. You may have to change the water in the bucket and wring the sponge out a few times. The goal is to clean the surface but not drag the slurry out of the voids. Let the slurry cure overnight.

12 PROCESS.

Use sandpaper to clean off any remaining residue and give the edges a final smoothing—this will help distinguish the veining.

▲ The stool that used to be a trash can.

▲ Water bubbles through a pump covered with river rocks.

WATER FEATURE
INTEGRAL COLOR WITH TWO SHADES

MODERATE

This project demonstrates how to use two colors in the same form. We used two concentrations of the same color because we wanted a subtle and natural finish, but you can use any color combination you like. We layered the two colors in the form, pouring one layer of colored concrete over another, allowing the two layers to mingle where they meet.

The form is made from two plastic serving bowls. The finished project measures 18 inches in diameter and is versatile—it can be a birdbath, water feature, or planter. We opted to make it a water feature by installing a pump which we covered with river rocks. You can adjust the sizes of the bowls as you like, but keep in mind that the thickness of the concrete wall should be a minimum of 1½ inches when you're using a commercial-grade concrete mix like Sakrete or Quikrete. If you want a water feature with a thinner wall and lighter weight, use a higher-performance mix.

▼ Some of the materials needed for this project.

1. Sakrete 5000 Plus Concrete Mix
2. Small bowl
3. Large bowl
4. Pigment
5. Melamine

MATERIALS

- Plastic bowl with an 18-inch diameter
- Plastic bowl with a 12-inch diameter
- Piece of melamine, approximately 20 × 20 inches
- Silicone caulk
- Rubber gloves
- Approximately ½ of an 80-lb. bag of Sakrete 5000 Plus Concrete Mix
- Water
- Two pigments (we used two concentrations of curry yellow)
- Plastic sheet
- Aquarium pump
- River rocks

TOOLS

- Drill
- 4- to 6-inch hole saw bit
- Tape measure or ruler
- Pencil
- Caulking gun
- Two 5-gallon mixing trays
- Margin trowel
- Small bucket or container
- Palm sander
- 80- to 120-grit sandpaper

1 CUT A HOLE IN THE LARGE BOWL.

Using a hole saw, cut a 4- to 6-inch hole in the center of the bottom of the larger bowl. Be sure that it's centered, because the circular shape of the hole will be the bottom of the water feature once it's turned over. We used a 6-inch hole saw to ensure that it is perfectly round, but if you are careful a jigsaw would work too. You'll pour the concrete into the form through the hole.

2 MAKE THE FORM. To assemble the form, use silicone to adhere the smaller bowl to the center of the melamine. The most efficient way to center the bowl is to use a tape measure or ruler to find the center of the melamine, mark the center with a pencil, center the bowl over the mark, and then outline the diameter of the bowl. Hold the bowl on the outline as you adhere it to the melamine. After you've adhered the smaller bowl, center the larger bowl over the smaller and adhere it to the melamine. Let the silicone cure for at least 30 minutes. Don't rush the wait time—if the silicone fails while you're casting the concrete, it will flow out from the bottom of the form.

▼ Cutting a hole through the bottom of the large bowl.

▼ Centering and adhering the smaller bowl to the melamine.

▼ Placing the larger bowl, being careful to center it over the smaller.

▼ Siliconing the larger bowl to the melamine.

▼ Casting the first color.

▼ Two layers of color, beginning to mix a little.

3. MIX TWO BATCHES OF CONCRETE.

Pour ¼ of the bag into one mixing tray and ¼ of the bag into another mixing tray and add water according to the manufacturer's directions, mixing by hand using a margin trowel. Mix thoroughly, then add a pigment to each tub.

4. CAST THE CONCRETE.

The color you cast first, which will land on the bottom of the form, will be at the top of the water feature once it's turned over when the project is finished. This may seem obvious, but overlooking this point has caused many a mishap while casting. Use a small bucket to pour the first layer of colored concrete into the form. Then, pour in a layer of the second color. We used multiple layers of the two colors, but feel free to use only two layers, or three, or however many you wish.

Once you've filled the form with concrete, vibrate it by tapping it lightly with a

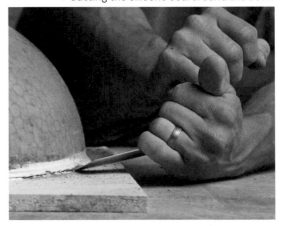
▼ Cutting the silicone seal around the bowl.

margin trowel or using an palm sander. The more you vibrate, the more the colors will mingle and mix causing the layers to lose their distinctiveness.

5 COVER THE FORM loosely with plastic and let it sit overnight on a flat surface to cure.

6 DEMOLD AND PROCESS. Before you remove the form, take a few minutes to clean up the concrete at the top of the form (the bottom of the bowl, where the hole is) with a margin trowel. The form will act as a guide as you smooth out any lumps or bumps left from the casting.

To separate the form from the melamine, cut the silicone seal around the outside of the bowl. Carefully slide a margin trowel between the concrete and the melamine and gently pry around the radius. You may have

▼ Pulling the melamine off the bowl.

▼ Popping out the inner bowl.

▼ Cracking the outer bowl.

▼ Carefully prying the outer bowl off.

▼ The bowl of the water feature has a nice glossy finish.

▼ Cleaning up the edge with a margin trowel before sanding.

▼ The finished cast with two mingled colors, ready to be made into a water feature.

to wiggle the trowel a little to break the form free from the melamine.

Once the melamine has been removed, use the trowel to lightly tap the plastic bowls until they break off. Be careful—broken plastic can be as sharp as glass and you do not want to damage the fresh concrete, not to mention your hands. (The inner bowl may pop out intact—the one we used did.) Lightly sand the edges of the water feature. Sand carefully and judiciously—if your water feature has a nice glossy finish you don't need to sand it.

7 INSTALL THE PUMP. Place the aquarium pump in the bowl and fill the bowl with river rocks to hide it and add some visual interest. Don't cover the pump outlet completely, because that's where the fountain of water will come from. Fill the water feature with water, plug in the pump, and enjoy the tranquil sounds of running water.

▲ Cover the pump with the river rocks.

▲ A rustic but modern addition to any garden.

BOARD-FORM FIRE PIT
INTEGRAL COLOR WITH PIGMENT STAIN

Gas fire pits are easy to use, and they can often be situated in spaces that aren't suitable for traditional wood fire pits. This project uses a casting technique called board form, where the texture of the wood form is cast onto the surface of the concrete. The form for the fire pit is made using construction-grade ¾-inch plywood because it has a strong wood-grain pattern that shows up nicely in the surface of the finished piece. The fire pit measures 24 × 18 × 12 inches. It has a shallow traylike space on top for lava rock or decorative glass and a gas burner, and a hollow underside that conceals the gas tank and line.

Color is added to the fire pit twice: first with an integral pigment that's mixed into the concrete, and again with a sprayed-on water-based stain that accentuates the grain pattern. The result is a durable, beautiful piece with a pattern that is inspired by nature yet very modern in appearance, perfect for gathering around and making memories with family and friends.

▼ Some of the materials needed for this project.

1. Plywood	**3.** Polystyrene foam	**5.** Petroleum jelly	**7.** Pigment
2. Sakrete 5000 Plus Concrete Mix	**4.** Packing tape	**6.** Water-based stain	

MATERIALS

- One piece of 2 × 20 × 14-inch polystyrene foam
- ¾ inch-thick construction-grade plywood:
    One 24 × 18-inch piece (for the base)
    Two 18 × 12¾-inch pieces (for the ends)
    Two 25½ × 12¾-inch pieces (for the sides)
- Silicone caulk
- 2-inch-long piece of 2-inch-wide PVC pipe
- 1¼- or 1½-inch screws
- Four pieces of 2 × 21 × 15-inch polystyrene foam
- Petroleum jelly
- Rubber gloves
- Two 80-lb. bags of Sakrete 5000 Plus Concrete Mix (or Quikrete 5000 Concrete Mix)
- Water
- Pigment (we used red, from Sakrete)
- Two pieces of scrap wood, approximately 30 inches long (for braces)
- Buddy Rhodes Water-Based Stain (we used black)
- Packing tape
- Plastic sheet
- Gas fire-pit burner kit
- Lava rocks or decorative glass

TOOLS

- Table saw or circular saw
- Tape measure
- Drill or driver and bit
- Caulking gun
- Drum mixer, or a wheelbarrow and hoe, or an extra-large bucket with a paddle mixer
- Small bucket
- Margin trowel
- Reciprocating saw (without the blade) or orbital sander
- Box cutter or carpenter's knife
- Spray bottle
- 80- to 120-grit sandpaper
- Two or three clean rags

1 ATTACH THE FOAM KNOCKOUT.

Center the $2 \times 20 \times 14$-inch piece of foam on the 24×18-inch piece of plywood, using a tape measure to ensure that it's centered, and adhere it in place with silicone. This will be the base of the form, and the foam knockout will create the tray that holds the lava rocks and burner. To ensure clean edges and a tight seal against seepage, apply silicone around the edges of the knockout.

2 BUILD THE FORM.

Screw the end and side pieces of the form to the base, predrilling the holes to ensure a tight-fitting form and minimize any leaking or moisture loss. Center the PVC pipe on the knockout and apply silicone around the outside of the bottom edge. The pipe creates an opening through which to run a gas line to the burner. It also acts as a spacer separating the two foam knockouts, allowing concrete to fill the space between the knockouts.

▼ Attaching the foam knockout to the base using silicone.

▼ Applying silicone around the edges of the knockout to ensure a strong seal.

▼ Assembling the sides of the form.

▼ Centering the PVC pipe before adhering it to the knockout.

▼ Taping the four pieces of foam together to create the second knockout.

3 MAKE THE SECOND KNOCKOUT.

Make the second knockout by taping together the four pieces of 2-inch-thick foam to create a single block that is 8 × 21 × 15 inches. Dry fit the knockout by placing it in the wood form to make sure it fits correctly. Once you're sure everything fits together, set aside the second knockout and coat the interior walls of the plywood form with a thin layer of petroleum jelly. The petroleum jelly prevents the plywood from swelling from the water in the concrete mix and helps the form come apart easily when you're demolding the piece.

▼ Applying a coat of petroleum jelly to the inside of the form.

4 MIX AND COLOR THE CONCRETE.

Pour the concrete into the drum mixer and add water according to the manufacturer's directions. Mix thoroughly. Once the concrete is well mixed, add the dry

▼ Pouring the concrete to the top edge of the PVC pipe.

▼ Placing the foam block in the center of the mold.

pigment and continue mixing. Be careful not to add too much water; the mix should flow freely out of a bucket.

5 **CAST THE CONCRETE.** Use a small bucket to pour enough concrete into the form to cover the first knockout and reach the top edge of the PVC pipe. Then center the second knockout in the form, place the two wood braces across the top of the form, and screw them onto the top edges of the form. The bracing will keep the foam block from floating up as you finish pouring the concrete.

Once the bracing is secure, finish filling the form with concrete. You may need to pack the concrete by hand. Lightly vibrate the form using a reciprocating saw (without the blade) or orbital sander to consolidate and release any air caught in the mix.

▼ Securing the braces over the foam block.

▼ Continuing to pour the walls of our form.

▼ Packing by hand makes sure there aren't any huge holes or air bubbles.

▼ Using a reciprocating saw to vibrate the form.

▼ Removing the braces.

6 **COVER THE FORM** loosely with plastic and let it sit overnight on a flat surface to cure.

7 **DEMOLD AND PROCESS.** Remove all the screws in the form and carefully pry off the plywood with a margin trowel. Once the form has been removed, lightly sand the edges of the fire pit if you like. Clean the surface with a rag, wiping off any residue left from the petroleum jelly. Using a box cutter and trowel, dig out the foam knockouts. Once you get the first chunk out, the rest will come out relatively easily.

▼ Carefully prying off the plywood.

▼ Removing the foam knockout.

▼ The tray will hold lava rocks and the burner.

8 **APPLY THE STAIN.** Set the fire pit on foam or some type of blocks (elevating the piece off the work surface makes it easier to apply the stain). Fill a spray bottle with the stain and coat the entire surface of the fire pit evenly. If you want a darker surface, apply a second coat of stain. (The stain can be reapplied multiple times to enhance or darken the surface.) Work the stain into the pores and texture of the concrete with a clean rag to bring out the pattern created by the plywood form.

9 **INSTALL THE BURNER.** Each burner kit is a little different, so follow the manufacturer's directions on the kit.

▼ Spraying the stain.

▼ Working the stain into the surface of the concrete.

▼ The wood texture is much more pronounced now.

▲ The planter and plants make an appealing contrast in textures.

LARGE OVAL PLANTER
INTEGRAL COLOR FOR VARIED COLOR VALUES

This large planter is perfect for a garden or patio because it can double as a table or seat. For color, we added white pigment to a gray-based concrete mix to explore the color possibilities of this type of Portland-cement-and-pigment combination. As you begin to develop your own color schemes and projects, it's important to understand the effect different mix designs can have on color.

The planter measures approximately 21 × 12 × 18, and the form used to make it is constructed from two cardboard tubes that are the same length but have different diameters. For the outer tube, we used a salvaged 55-gallon drum that once held a type of liquid and had a waterproof finish on the inside, which gave the planter a nice glossy finish. The inner tube is a commercial concrete form tube that can be found at most hardware stores and is made specifically for casting concrete.

We were intrigued by the planter's appearance once it was finished. The small, varied white striations are the result of using the white pigment with a gray-based concrete mix. We suspect (because even as professionals, we don't always have all the answers; that is the beauty of working with concrete) that this particular finish occurred due to the slick, waterproof interior of the outer tube combined with the pigment and admixtures found

▼ Some of the materials needed for this project.

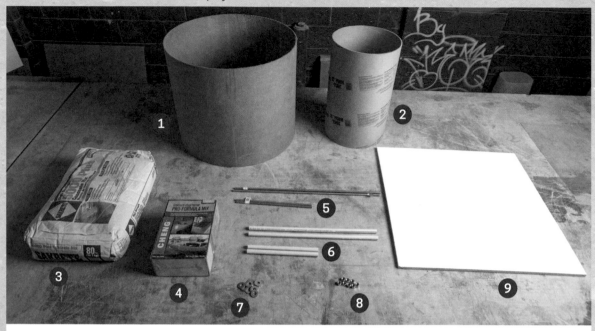

1. Large cardboard tube

2. Small cardboard tube

3. Sakrete 5000 Plus Concrete Mix

4. Cheng Pro-Formula Mix

5. All-thread rods

6. PVC pipe

7. Washers

8. Nuts

9. Melamine

MATERIALS

- One 18- to 19-inch-long concrete form tube with a 12-inch diameter (we used a Sakrete tube)
- One 18- to 19-inch-long concrete form tube or cardboard tube with a 21-inch diameter (we salvaged a cardboard tube from a 55-gallon drum)
- Two 12-inch lengths of ⅜-inch all-thread rod
- Two 24-inch lengths of ⅜-inch all-thread rod
- Eight ⅜-inch washers
- Eight ⅜-inch nuts
- Two 10-inch lengths of PVC pipe with a ½-inch diameter
- Two 18-inch lengths of PVC pipe with a ½-inch diameter
- 30 × 30-inch piece of ¾-inch melamine
- Silicone caulk
- Rubber gloves
- Four 80-lb. bags of Sakrete 5000 Plus Concrete Mix
- Water
- Three packages of Cheng Pro-Formula Mix (we used platinum)
- Plastic sheet

TOOLS

- Ruler or tape measure
- Felt marker or pencil
- Drill
- ⅜-inch bit
- Caulking gun
- Drum mixer (or a wheelbarrow and hoe)
- Small bucket or container
- Box cutter or carpenter's knife
- Margin trowel
- 80- to 120-grit sandpaper

in Cheng Pro-Formula Mix. Using an unsealed form probably would not have yielded the same results. And finally, we consider the bugholes in the planter, which occur naturally, to be an attractive trait, so if your planter has them too, don't be dismayed—they're not blemishes. Bugholes and striation lines found in wet-cast concrete such as this should be considered a concrete delicacy.

1 PREPARE THE TUBES. Rather than casting a conventional round planter, we wanted to bring an unusual dimension to this project. Manipulating the tubes into an oval shape is an easy way to do this.

Begin by drawing a line up one side of the smaller tube. Use a ruler to help you draw a straight line from end to end. Draw another line up the opposite side of the tube, directly across from the first line. The lines divide the tube in half. On one line mark two spots 5 inches from each end of the tube and do the same on the other line, making marks 5 inches from each end. Drill a ⅜-inch hole into each of the four points you've marked.

▼ Marking the guide lines, one on each side of the smaller tube.

▼ The hash marks indicate where to drill the holes in the smaller tube.

▼ Drilling the holes to draw the all-thread rods through.

▼ Fitting the all-thread rods and PVC pipe inside the smaller tube.

▼ The tightened nuts force the tube into an oval shape.

2 PREPARE THE ALL-THREAD RODS.

Place a washer and nut on one end of a 12-inch-long all-thread rod. Draw the other end of the all-thread rod through one of the lower holes, feed it into the 10-inch-long PVC pipe, and pass it through the lower hole on the opposite side, threading on another washer and nut. You may need to get some extra help for this part—one person squeezing the tube while the other threads on the nut. The ends of the all-thread rod will jut out from the tube, and there should be a washer and nut on each end on the outside of the tube. Repeat with the other 12-inch-long all-thread rod and 10-inch-long PVC pipe. Tighten the washers and nuts to the PVC pipes. The pipes act as a guide for the all-thread rods and as spacers for the cardboard tube, preventing it from being squeezed smaller by the concrete.

Repeat the process with the larger tube, except don't divide the tube in half with the penciled lines; instead, make both lines a few inches off center to allow enough room for the smaller tube to fit inside the larger tube once the all-thread rods are drawn through the larger tube. If the all-thread rods span the larger tube through the center, there won't be enough room for the smaller tube to fit inside. Place the smaller tube inside the larger tube to see where the lines should be drawn. There should be approximately 1 inch of space between the PVC pipes in the larger tube and the smaller tube once the smaller tube is placed inside the larger tube.

3 ADHERE THE TUBES TO THE BASE. Before adhering the tubes to the melamine, dry fit them to check their positioning on the melamine. Using silicone, adhere the smaller tube first. Once the small tube is attached, carefully place the larger tube around it and adhere it in place. Use the silicone generously, because it's holding the form together. If the silicone fails, the concrete will leak out at the bottom of the form. Because we are using so much concrete in this form and the pressure will be considerable, we strongly recommend letting the silicone reach its full cure before casting the concrete.

▼ Make sure there is clearance between the smaller tube and the PVC pipes in the larger tube.

▼ Silicone the tubes to the melamine base of the form.

▼ Carefully pouring the concrete into the form by hand.

▼ The finished pour ready to be covered in plastic.

▼ Removing the nuts and washers.

▼ Carefully cutting the cardboard with a knife.

4 MIX AND POUR THE CONCRETE.

Empty the bags of Sakrete and the packages of Cheng Pro-Formula into the mixer and add water according to the directions on the Cheng Pro-Formula package. Mix until the concrete has a fluid consistency that can be easily poured.

Using a small bucket or container, carefully pour the mix into the larger tube only (the smaller tube stays empty; it creates the space for a plant) and lightly tap around the sides with your hands to consolidate the mix and eliminate any air bubbles. The form is relatively fragile, since we are only using silicone to hold it together, so keep this in mind as you vibrate and tap. Volume in a form like this can be difficult to calculate, so if the concrete doesn't fill the form to the rim, don't worry about it.

5 **COVER THE FORM** loosely with plastic and let it sit overnight on a flat surface to cure.

6 **DEMOLD AND PROCESS.** After removing the plastic sheet, use a knife or trowel to gently score the silicone around the bottom of the outer tube. Remove the nuts and washers from the outer tube. Pull the all-thread rods in the larger tube out of the PVC pipes. (The all-thread rods in the smaller tube will remain there; they'll be covered with soil once your plant is in place.) Once the all-thread rods are removed, use a box cutter or knife to cut the cardboard tubes and remove them. Lightly sand the edges if they need smoothing.

▼ Peeling the form away from the planter.

▼ Removing the all-thread rods.

▼ The finished piece with bugholes and striations.

▲ The perfect place for a little afternoon fun.

CHILD'S CHAIR
INTEGRAL COLOR IN ANY HUE

This project is a modern chair for the discerning child. It's as visually entertaining as it is useful; it works beautifully outdoors but is equally at home indoors too. The color is integral—it's added to the concrete mix.

We used melamine for the form because it gives the concrete a smooth finish, perfect for a chair. The foam knockout for this project is as critical to the finished piece as the melamine. While the melamine provides the structure, the foam provides the shape that turns the cube into a chair. The chair measures approximately $12 \times 12 \times 12$ inches and is heavy enough that children can't turn it over or move it around much.

▼ Some of the materials needed for this project.

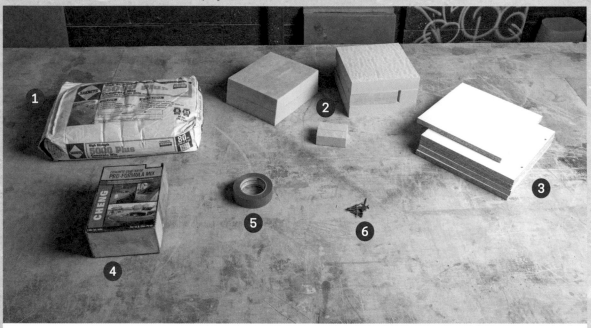

1. Sakrete 5000 Plus Concrete Mix
2. Polystyrene foam
3. Melamine
4. Cheng Pro-Formula Mix
5. Packing tape
6. Screws

MATERIALS

- ¾-inch melamine:

    Four 12¾ × 12¾-inch pieces (for the sides)

    One 12 × 12-inch piece (for the bottom)

    Two 15 × 3-inch pieces (for bracing)

- 1¼- to 1½-inch screws
- Silicone caulk
- Polystyrene foam:

    Two 2 × 10½ × 9-inch pieces (for the seat block)

    Two 4 × 1½ × 1½-inch pieces (for the handles)

    Three 2 × 10 × 10-inch pieces (for the second block)

    Four scrap pieces approximately 1-inch thick (to use as shims)

- Packing tape

- Approximately ½ to ⅔ of an 80-lb. bag of Sakrete 5000 Plus Concrete Mix
- One partial package of Cheng Pro-Formula Mix (we used indigo)
- Water
- Plastic sheet

TOOLS

- Table saw or circular saw
- Power drill or driver and bit
- Caulking gun
- Drum mixer or wheelbarrow and hoe
- Rubber gloves
- Bucket
- Margin trowel
- 80- to 120-grit sandpaper

1 **BUILD THE FORM.** Attach three of the 12¾ × 12¾-inch side pieces to the 12 × 12-inch bottom piece, predrilling the holes to ensure a solidly constructed form (the fourth side is left open for the time being so that you can easily place the foam knockout inside the form). Using the bottom as a guide when you attach the sides helps keep the form square and tight. Silicone the interior seams.

▼ Screwing together the form.

2 **MAKE THE KNOCKOUT FOR THE SEAT BLOCK.** A large foam knockout, or seat block, creates the sitting area for the chair. Make the seat block by gluing the two 2 × 10½ × 9-inch pieces of polystyrene foam together with silicone. On the 10½-inch side, cut an angle of 10 degrees; this sloped side will create the backrest of the chair. The foam we used had an uneven texture that would show up in the cast, so we sanded all the sides to make them smooth (if the foam you're using is smooth, you may not need to do this step). Center a 4 × 1½ × 1½-inch piece of foam on one 9-inch side of the seat block and flush with the longer side (see illustration), adhere it in place with silicone, and do the same with the other piece on the other side of the seat block. These two small pieces will make the handles that are inset in the chair. Once the knockouts for the handles are secure, apply silicone around the seams for the handle knockouts and the seat block and let it dry for 30 minutes.

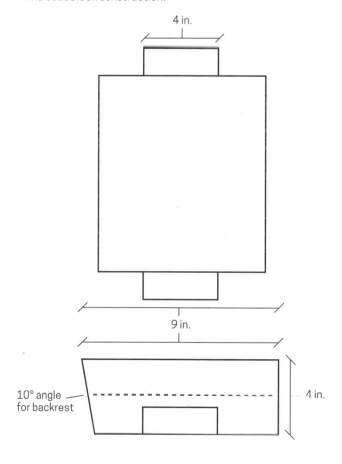
▼ The seat block construction.

4 in.

9 in.

10° angle for backrest

4 in.

▼ Sanding down the foam.

3 PLACE THE SEAT BLOCK IN THE FORM.
After the silicone has dried, use silicone to adhere the seat block inside the form with the knockouts for the chair's handles facing up. The handle knockouts should touch both sides of the form. To finish building the form, screw on the fourth 12¾ × 12¾-inch side of melamine.

4 BUILD ANOTHER FOAM BLOCK.
This block of foam fills up space inside the form so that the finished chair isn't a solid, heavy block of concrete. Tape the three pieces of 2 × 10 × 10-inch foam together to make a single block that is 6 inches thick and set it aside.

▼ A smooth, consistent surface.

▼ Centering the knockouts for the handles on the seat block.

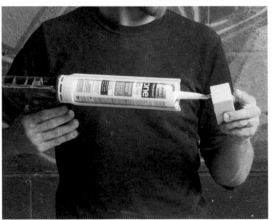
▼ Silicone the knockouts for the handles to the seat block.

5 **MIX THE CONCRETE.** Mix the Sakrete 5000 Plus and Cheng Pro-Formula Mix with enough water to make a consistency that will flow from the bucket. With Cheng Pro-Formula Mix in this mix you won't need as much water as usual, so keep an eye on the consistency so that you don't add too much water to the mix.

6 **CAST THE CONCRETE.** Pour the concrete into the form, covering the seat block with a 1-inch layer of concrete. Vibrate the form by hand using a trowel or hammer to level out the concrete, then place the second foam block into the form and center it in the space. Screw the two brace pieces across the top of the form and place the foam shims under the braces to hold the foam block down (otherwise the block may float up while you finish pouring the concrete).

▼ Positioning the foam knockouts for the chair's handles.

▼ Applying silicone to the seams around the knockouts for the chair's handles.

▼ Silicone the seat block into the form.

▼ Tape the foam together as tight as possible.

▼ Pour in enough concrete to cover the seat block about an inch.

▼ The second foam block is centered in the form.

▼ The braces are in place and the shims are holding the knockout tight.

7 FINISH THE POUR. Finish filling the form with concrete, covering the foam block (it will remain embedded in the concrete permanently). You may need to pack the concrete into the side areas by hand. Once it's full, vibrate the form by hand using a trowel or hammer, or use an orbital sander, to work out any air bubbles. If you want to keep some air bubbles to add texture and visual interest, then vibrate less; this is purely an aesthetic decision.

▼ Finishing the pour.

8 **COVER THE FORM** loosely with plastic and let it sit overnight on a flat surface to cure.

9 **DEMOLD AND FINISH.** Remove all the screws and carefully pry apart the form using a margin trowel. When you're removing the foam, don't be afraid to cut and break it into pieces. This is probably the only way you will be able to get it out. You can leave the shim pieces in place or dig them out. If you leave them in place, sand them down so that they're flush with the bottom of the chair. Finish the edges and corners by lightly sanding them.

▼ The concrete should come up to the bottom of the braces.

▼ Removing the form.

▼ Removing the foam knockouts.

▼ Ready for some sitting.

▲ Style and function: fire on one side and firewood storage on the other.

WOOD-BURNING FIRE PIT
INTEGRAL COLOR WITH CONCRETE JOINERY

This handsome fire pit is the perfect excuse to get together with family and friends and enjoy drinks or s'mores. The fire pit measures $34 \times 34 \times 12$ inches and consists of three pieces of concrete that interlock to form the shape of an H. One side is designed for the fire and the other side stores firewood.

Concrete's longevity declines when it repeatedly comes into contact with open flames, so we recommend using a firebox or fireplace grate on the wood-burning side to take the brunt of the abuse. Fireboxes and grates can be found at home-improvement stores, or you could have one built by a local metal shop like we did. Building the form for this project is challenging, so if you're a novice in the workshop we recommend gaining some experience by undertaking some of the easier projects in this book before tackling this one.

The mix of pigments and chemical additives in Cheng Pro-Formula Mix upgrades the Sakrete 5000 Plus Concrete Mix to something more suitable for decorative concrete projects. Cheng Pro-Formula Mix calls for one package per bag of concrete; however, we wanted a less-saturated color so we used a little less than three packages instead of four. If you prefer a richer, more saturated color, use four packages of Cheng Pro-Formula Mix.

▼ Some of the materials needed for this project.

1. Cheng Pro-Formula

2. Melamine

3. Water

4. Polystyrene foam

5. Sakrete 5000 Plus
   Concrete Mix

MATERIALS

- ¾-inch melamine:

   Six 34 × 12-inch pieces (for the sides)

   Six 12 × 4½-inch pieces (for the ends)

   Three 34 × 4½-inch pieces (for the bottoms)

- 1¼- or 1½-inch screws

- 1½ × 12 × 24-inch polystyrene foam

- Silicone caulk

- Rubber gloves

- Four 80-lb. bags of Sakrete 5000 Plus
  Concrete Mix

- Three packages of Cheng Pro-Formula Mix (we
  used amethyst)

- Water

- Plastic sheet

TOOLS

- Table saw or circular saw

- Drill or driver and bit

- Caulking gun

- Handsaw

- Drum mixer, or power mixer and bucket, or
  wheelbarrow and hoe

- Small bucket

- Tape measure or ruler

- Box cutter or carpenter's knife

- 80- to 120-grit sandpaper

- Margin trowel

- Reciprocating saw or orbital sander

- Six quick clamps that can open to 6 inches

1 **BUILD THE FORMS.** This project requires three forms, which are identical in shape and size but have different knockouts. Build the first form by screwing the bottom and end pieces to one of the 34 × 12 inch side pieces, leaving off the other side piece. Leaving one side open for the time being gives you plenty of open space to work in when you attach the foam knockouts. Remember to predrill the screw holes in the melamine; predrilling creates a tighter form and reduces the likelihood of splitting the melamine. Build the remaining two forms the same way, leaving off the second side piece.

2 **MAKE THE KNOCKOUTS.** The knockouts create the voids that allow the concrete pieces to slip into one another to make the H shape, so their accuracy is of the utmost importance. All the cuts need to be straight, and all the corners need to be square. Because the concrete blocks are cast at 3 inches thick, the knockouts need to be 3³⁄₁₆ inches wide to allow a little bit of room for assembling the three finished concrete pieces.

Using the handsaw, make four knockouts, two measuring 3 × 3³⁄₁₆ × 6 inches and two that are L-shaped. See the illustration for the dimensions.

▼ Building the forms.

▼ Dimensions for the L-shaped knockouts.

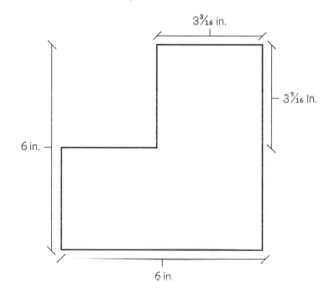

3³⁄₁₆ in.

3³⁄₁₆ in.

6 in.

6 in.

▼ The L-shaped knockouts face out.

3 ATTACH THE KNOCKOUTS. Using
silicone, attach the two L-shaped knockouts, facing out, to the bottom corners in one form, and place the rectangular knockouts in the center top in each of the other two forms, flush with the edge of the form. Apply silicone to the back of the knockouts to adhere them, and then run a bead around the forms' seams to prevent leakage. Then screw on the last side and let the silicone cure.

▼ Attaching the knockouts.

4 MIX THE CONCRETE. Because of the
size of this project we used a drum mixer, but it's completely feasible to mix the concrete in a wheelbarrow using a hoe or in a large bucket with an electric mixer. Combine the Sakrete 5000 Plus Concrete Mix and the Cheng Pro-Formula together in the drum mixer (or other container) and

▼ Carefully placing the knockouts.

▼ Waterproofing the form's seams.

add water according to the instructions on the Cheng Pro-Formula Mix packaging. The Cheng Pro-Formula Mix changes the amount of water needed, so add water sparingly and be sure to mix thoroughly between additions of water until you have a consistency that will flow freely out of a bucket but is not sloppy or sloshy.

5 **CAST THE CONCRETE.** This is the easy part! Use a small bucket to pour the mix into the three forms until they're filled to the top edge. Using a reciprocating saw or orbital sander, lightly vibrate the forms to release any air bubbles and consolidate the concrete. After vibrating, top off the forms with a little more concrete if needed. Next, apply clamps across the top of each form to prevent pressure from the wet concrete from making the side walls

▼ The forms with the knockouts in place and ready to cast.

▼ Pouring concrete can be messy.

▼ Vibrating with a reciprocating saw.

▼ Applying clamps to ensure each form's 3-inch thickness.

▼ Fresh concrete.

▼ Pulling out a foam knockout.

▼ Our pieces ready for assembly.

bow—if this happens the final pieces will not fit together. Tighten the clamps firmly but not so much that they make the width of the form smaller—the 3-inch width of concrete inside the form should remain consistent.

6 **COVER THE FORMS** loosely with plastic and let them sit overnight on a flat surface to cure.

7 **DEMOLD THE CURED CONCRETE.** Remove the screws and carefully pry off the melamine using a margin trowel or other tool. Lightly sand the edges of the three pieces to remove any rough spots or sharp corners. Even though melamine supplies a smooth finish, it is normal and even desirable to have some bugholes and layering (the striations from the different pours of concrete into the forms); they add to the unique character of each piece. Next, remove the foam knockouts. Here, too, a margin trowel works wonders.

8 **ASSEMBLE THE PIECES.** Though concrete is incredibly strong, the surface of freshly cured concrete is susceptible to chipping, so handle the pieces with care while you're assembling them. The longer you can let the concrete set before assembling the fire pit, the stronger the concrete will be and the less chance you'll have of chipping the edges. Carefully fit the pieces together (you may need to have someone help you) and then install the fire box or grate.

▼ Carefully sliding the pieces together.

▼ Everything fitting as it should.

▼ The firebox set in place.

▲ Just swinging in the breeze on a charming two-color swing.

GARDEN SWING
INTEGRAL COLOR WITH MULTIPLE HUES

The classic garden swing is given a modern update in this concrete version with a curved seat. The soft colors reflect the innocence a swing evokes, yet the design is quite contemporary. This project explores the use of two integral colors combined in one form to create a very distinctive two-toned seat. The colors bleed into each other where they meet, creating a soft segue from one color to the next.

The design of the swing calls for using a heavy-duty reinforcement in the form of rebar to make the swing structurally sound and support the weight of the person sitting on the swing. The finished swing measures 24 × 10 × 3 inches.

▼ Some of the materials needed for this project.

1. Cheng Pro-Formula Mix   **3.** Melamine   **5.** Polystyrene foam   **7.** Screws

2. Laminate   **4.** Sakrete 5000 Plus Concrete Mix   **6.** Rebar

MATERIALS

- ¾-inch melamine:

    One 24 × 10-inch piece (for the base)

    Two 10 × 3¾-inch pieces (for the short sides of the form)

    Two 25½ × 3¾-inch pieces (for the long sides of the form)

    Two 10 × 1-inch pieces (for the middle supports)

    Two 10 × ½-inch pieces (for the end supports)

- 1¼- or 1½-inch screws

- Laminate:

    One 10 × 25-inch piece

    Two 24 × 3-inch pieces

- Four 2 × 2 × 2-inch pieces of polystyrene foam

- Two ½ × 22-inch pieces of rebar

- Silicone caulk

- Rubber gloves

- ⅓ to ½ of an 80-lb. bag of Sakrete 5000 Plus Concrete Mix

- Two packages of Cheng Pro-Formula Mix (we used approximately ¼ package each of olive and wine)

- Water

- Plastic sheet

- Two lengths of rope to hang the swing

TOOLS

- Table saw or circular saw

- Tape measure

- Pencil

- Power drill or driver

- ½-inch drill bit

- Caulking gun

- Two 15-gallon mixing trays

- Margin trowel

- Hammer

- 80- to 120-grit sandpaper

1 **BUILD THE FORM.** Using a table saw or a circular saw, cut a groove down the length of the long side of the two 10 × 3¾-inch pieces of melamine, ¾ inch from the bottom. The groove will be used to hold the piece of laminate that creates the curve on the seat of the swing.

Screw the side pieces to the base of the form, leaving one long side open for the time being, and remembering to predrill the holes in the melamine. Position the two 10 × 1-inch support pieces next to each other in the center of the base and screw them into place. Position the 10 × ½-inch support pieces toward the ends, 3 to 4 inches from each end, and screw them into place. These pieces will support the weight of the mix so that it doesn't deform the curve of the laminate. Slide the 10 × 25 inch piece of laminate into the grooves—it will flex up, creating the curve in the seat. When you are happy with the fit, apply silicone to all the seams to seal the form.

▼ The groove sits just above the base of the form.

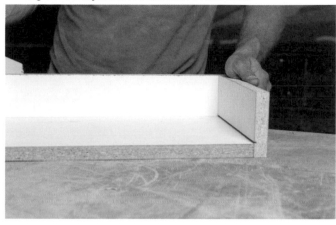

▼ Attaching the short sides of the form to the base.

▼ Installing the support pieces: two in the middle and one near each end.

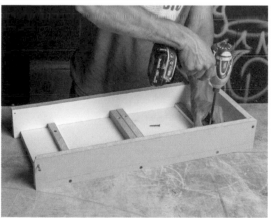

▼ Flexing the laminate to fit into the grooves.

▼ Applying silicone to the seams.

2 PREPARE THE FOAM BLOCKS.

The 2 × 2-inch foam cubes pull double-duty by providing support for the rebar during casting and as knockouts creating four holes in the swing to thread rope through. Designate a top and a bottom for the cubes, then lightly round the four edges of the cubes with sandpaper (rounding the corners makes it easier to dig the cubes out later, and it also gives the holes in the swing a more attractive appearance). The top and bottom sides do not need to be sanded.

▼ Sanding the foam knockouts.

3 ASSEMBLE THE FOAM BLOCKS AND REBAR.

The pieces of rebar reinforce the concrete. They're positioned at the top of the form (which is the bottom of the swing) to provide support for the weight of the person sitting on the swing. It is imperative that you position the structural reinforcement in the correct part of the form. Drill a ½-inch hole through each foam

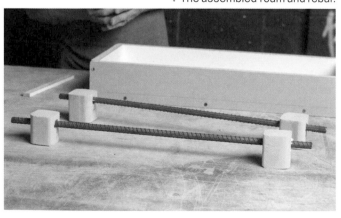

▼ The assembled foam and rebar.

▼ Marking the placement of the foam knockouts in the form.

block 1½ inches from the bottom. Slide one piece of foam onto each end of the pieces of rebar, about 2 inches from the ends. Adhere the foam in place on the rebar with silicone. Last, stand the two 24 × 3-inch pieces of laminate on their side between the foam supports in the center of the form. They don't need to be secured to the form—they'll keep the two colors separate as you're casting the concrete and then they'll be removed.

4 **MIX THE CONCRETE.** This piece requires a consistency that is less liquid—it should be stiffer and able to sit solidly on a trowel. Divide the Sakrete 5000 Plus Concrete Mix and Cheng Pro-Formula between two mixing trays, one color in each tub, and add water slowly as you mix. Keep close tabs on the consistency so that you don't add too much water.

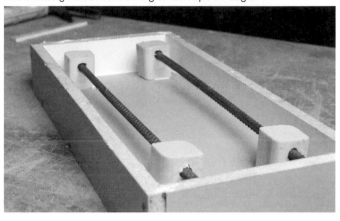

▼ The knockouts perform two tasks: supporting the rebar and creating holes in the swing to run rope through.

▼ The laminated pieces act as temporary dividers while the two colors of concrete are being cast.

▼ Packing the mix with a margin trowel.

▼ The laminate dividers have been removed.

▼ The smoothed casting, ready to cure.

▼ Removing the melamine form. You can see the small curve in the swing created by the flexed piece of laminate.

▼ The foam removed, revealing the pieces of rebar.

5 **CAST THE CONCRETE.** Fill the three sections of the form using a margin trowel, taking care to maintain a clear division between the colors using the pieces of laminate. Once the sections are filled, pull the laminate out and gently vibrate the form by tapping on it with a hammer. When you are finished vibrating, smooth the top of the cast with a trowel. Don't worry if the colors mix at this point; if they do, it will only happen near the bottom of the mold.

6 **COVER THE FORM LOOSELY** with plastic and let it sit overnight on a flat surface to cure.

7 **DEMOLD AND PROCESS.** Remove all the screws in the form and carefully pull off the melamine. Any bugholes left in the sides are expected and add to the beauty and texture of the piece. Remove the foam knockouts. Because they are small and have rebar threaded through them, the easiest way to dig them out is by drilling them out using a ½-inch bit. Clean up the foam residue with your hands. Sand the edges of the swing with 80- to 120-grit sandpaper.

8 **HANG THE SWING.** When you are ready to hang the swing, be sure to run the rope around the rebar and not the concrete. The rebar distributes the weight throughout the swing and protects the rope from unnecessary wear.

▲ Adding a sense of romance and whimsy to the garden.

▲ Pull up some chairs around the table on a cool evening in the garden.

CAST-IN-PLACE SIDE TABLE
INTEGRAL COLOR WITH TROWEL FINISH

The color and visual texture of this side table is enhanced by a troweling technique that brings out a natural burnished finish in the concrete. It's a technique that can yield rich, dappled coloring reminiscent of leather and, with practice, can become a signature finish for crafters working with concrete. There's a bit of a learning curve to perfecting this technique, but don't let that stop you from trying. Once mastered, it can be used on its own or in conjunction with pigments or stains, opening up a world of possibility for finishing concrete.

The table measures 18 × 24 × 18 inches and is cast right-side up—in other words, the form is built right-side up, instead of upside-down, and the table-top will be finished and troweled. Casting right-side up requires more time and patience during the casting process, because you have to wait for the concrete to set throughout the troweling process. Allow the better part of a day to finish the cast. The legs are an integral part of the design of this project: they extend a few inches beyond the edge of the table, creating two small ledges and adding visual interest and depth to the overall piece.

▼ Some of the materials needed for this project.

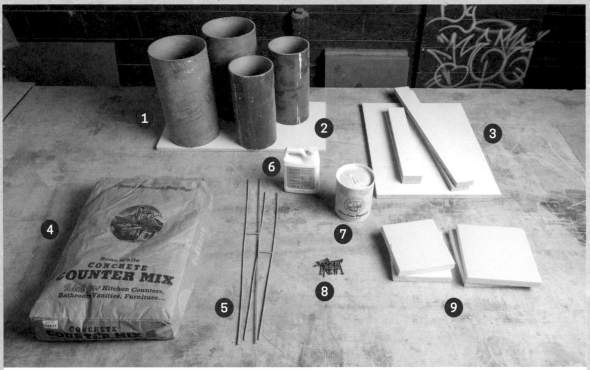

1. Cardboard tubes

2. Melamine

3. Melamine

4. Buddy Rhodes Bone White Concrete Counter Mix

5. Masonry ladder wire

6. Water reducer

7. Pigment

8. Screws

9. Polystyrene foam

MATERIALS

- Concrete form tubes:

  Two 6-inch diameter × 13-inch-long tubes

  Two 8-inch diameter × 15-inch-long tubes

- Polystyrene foam:

  Two 1 × 8 × 8-inch pieces

  Two 1 × 10 × 10-inch pieces

- ¾-inch melamine:

  One 14 × 27-inch piece (for the base of the leg forms)

  One 18 × 24-inch piece (for the base of the tabletop form)

  Two 26½ × 2¾-inch pieces (for the long sides of the tabletop form)

  Two 18 × 2¾- inch pieces (for the short sides of the tabletop form)

- Silicone caulk

- 1¼- or 1½-inch screws

- Rubber gloves

- Two 70-lb. bags of Buddy Rhodes Bone White Concrete Counter Mix

- Buddy Rhodes Ultra-Fine Pigment (we used a color called universe)

- Water

- Water reducer

- Two 22-inch lengths of ⅜-inch masonry ladder wire

- Plastic sheet

TOOLS

- Table saw or circular saw
- Pen or pencil
- Caulking gun
- Power drill or driver
- Tape measure
- Box cutter or carpenter's knife
- Mixing tray
- Paddle mixer
- Small bucket
- Reciprocating saw or orbital sander
- 24-inch-long 2 × 4 screed board
- Margin trowel
- Resin or wood trowel
- Steel trowel
- 80- to 120-grit sandpaper

1 BUILD THE FORMS FOR THE LEGS.

Trace the diameter of one of the smaller casting tubes onto each of the two 8-inch pieces of foam and cut out the circles with a box cutter or carpenter's knife. Sand the edges and sides of the circles lightly to smooth them out. Repeat with the larger tubes and the 10 × 10-inch pieces of foam. Adhere the smaller casting tubes to the 14 × 27-inch piece of melamine with silicone. Center the larger casting tubes over the smaller ones and adhere them to the melamine. Set a small foam circle on the top of each small casting tube, adhere them in place with silicone, and let dry. The foam circles will prevent concrete from getting into the smaller tubes.

▼ Outlining the smaller tubes on the foam.

▼ Adhering the smaller tubes to the melamine base.

▼ Centering the larger tubes around the smaller tubes.

▼ Adhering the large tubes to the melamine base.

▼ Capping the smaller tubes with the circles of foam, using silicone to adhere them in place.

2 BUILD THE FORM FOR THE TABLE-TOP.

Screw the side pieces to the 18 × 24-inch base of the form. (Predrill the holes, as usual, to create a tighter construction.) Apply silicone to the inside seams of the form and let it dry to the touch, about 30 minutes.

3 MAKE THE FOAM KNOCKOUTS.

The knockouts create the insets on the underside of the tabletop for the legs to fit into. They're made by cutting off a piece of the large foam circles to create a flat side. Take one of the large foam circles and measure 5 inches in from one side. (We find that this works best if you hold the circle against a stable flat edge and measure 5 inches in from that side.) Mark the 5-inch point with a pencil, and draw a line from the top of the circle to the bottom through the 5-inch mark. Cut along the line, discard the smaller piece (or save it for another use), then position the larger piece along one of the long sides of the form 3 inches from one end, and use silicone to adhere it in place. Apply silicone around the rounded edge too. Repeat with the other large foam circle and position it on the opposite long side 3 inches from the other end. Let dry for 30 minutes.

4 MIX THE CONCRETE. While the silicone dries, pour the concrete and pigment into a mixing tray. Slowly add water while mixing—the mix should be somewhat stiff because you will be using your hands to pack the concrete into the forms. If the mix is too loose, the concrete won't be as strong, and you'll have to wait longer to start the troweling process described in step 7.

5 CAST THE TABLETOP. Cast the tabletop by tightly packing the form about one-third full. Gently press the two pieces of ladder wire into the surface of the concrete so that they are positioned toward the bottom of the form and at least ½ inch from each side of the form (far enough from the sides so that there's no risk of their protruding from the edge of the table), then fill the form to the top with concrete. Once the form is full, run the screed across the surface using a side-to-side motion to flatten out any irregularities and remove excess mix, making the surface as flat as possible. You may need to repeat this process several times. When you are satisfied that the surface is level, go over it lightly with a resin or wood trowel. This stage brings the cream, or liquid parts of the cement, to the surface, which is the material you will work and burnish for the finished effect.

▼ Screwing the side pieces to the base for the tabletop form.

▼ Measuring 5 inches in, using a flat edge for stability.

▼ Using a box cutter to cut one of the large foam circles.

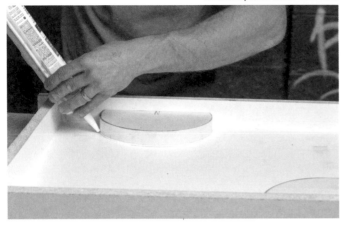

▼ Positioning the knockouts and adhering them in place with silicone.

6 CAST THE LEGS. Double-check the silicone to be sure it has dried completely before you begin casting the legs. The silicone is the only thing attaching the tubes to the melamine, so it's imperative that it's dry and the tubes are secure. Add the water reducer to the remaining concrete and mix thoroughly. You should notice the mix loosening up and the concrete flowing more easily. Begin pouring the mix into the legs using a small bucket. Vibrate the forms occasionally with a reciprocating saw or an orbital sander. The vibrations will work the mix down the leg forms, ensuring a solid cast. Fill both leg forms to the top and use a trowel to smooth the top, as you did with the surface of the tabletop. Let both the tabletop and the legs sit for 45 to 60 minutes before starting the next step.

▼ Packing the tabletop form with concrete by hand.

▼ Placing the masonry ladder wire.

▼ Running the screed across the top.

7 **TROWEL THE TABLETOP SURFACE AND TOPS OF THE LEGS.** This is the fun part, although it requires patience. When the surface of the tabletop is firm to the touch and doesn't stick to your fingers, it's time to trowel. The proper way to use a float or trowel is to slightly lift the leading edge as you move it across the surface. This prevents the trowel from gouging or digging into the surface. Using the steel trowel, work over the surface of the concrete using a combination of long sweeping strokes and shorter side-to-side strokes. You'll also be able to fill any dips in the concrete with the cream you're working up on the surface, creating a flat top. As you work you will notice a change in the surface as it starts to burnish. Darker areas will form and the concrete will take on a deep, mottled look. Spray the trowel with water occasionally to help it slide over the concrete more easily and pull small particles of cement up, but do not add too much—excess water will weaken the surface of the concrete. When the surface is smooth and you are happy with the tabletop's mottled and burnished appearance, stop. Repeat this step on the tops of the legs.

▼ Using a resin float to smooth the surface.

▼ Vibrating occasionally as we cast.

▼ The legs leveled and floated.

▼ Smoothing the surface with the steel float.

8 **COVER THE FORMS** loosely with plastic and let them sit overnight on a flat surface to cure.

Take care not to let the plastic touch or lay on top of the troweled surface as it might discolor the surface.

9 **DEMOLD THE CONCRETE AND PROCESS.** To demold the tabletop, unscrew and pry off the melamine pieces. Once the melamine is removed, dig out the foam knockouts. To demold the legs, carefully cut the cardboard tubes and peel them off. The inner tubes with the foam tops will remain embedded in the table's legs. If you like, sand the corners and edges of the concrete pieces with sandpaper.

▼ Working the cream up to the surface.

▼ Troweling the legs.

▼ Beginning to burnish the surface and develop texture.

10 **ASSEMBLE THE TABLE.** Slip each leg into one of the insets underneath the tabletop. About three inches or so of the legs will extend past the edge of the table, creating not only a small ledge but also visual interest and depth.

▼ Removing the melamine.

▼ Peeling away the cardboard tube.

▼ Top and legs assembled.

▲ The perfect place for a bike.

BIKE STAND
INTEGRAL COLOR WITH INLAID OBJECT

This bike stand has a simple and elegant design that is easy to use and will add a touch of industrial-chic to your porch or next to your garden shed. The design also offers an opportunity to add a small embellishment, such as a bicycle cog. Bugholes and the color variations that occur naturally with each cast are among the many beautiful aspects of wet-cast concrete. If your bike stand has a lot of bugholes, relish in this perfectly imperfect material.

Building the form is the most complicated part of this project—the angles of the melamine pieces make the project a bit intimidating, but once the pieces are cut, they fit together just like every other form in this book. Take a few minutes to review the illustrations before you begin. All the cuts are either at a 90-degree angle or a 45-degree angle—neither is terribly difficult. If you are handy with a saw, give this project a try. Otherwise, we recommend working on a few of the easier projects in this book first to gain some experience. This project is sizable enough to justify using a concrete mixer, but a wheelbarrow and hoe would work too. The stand measures approximately 23½ × 23½ × 4 inches.

▼ Some of the materials needed for this project.

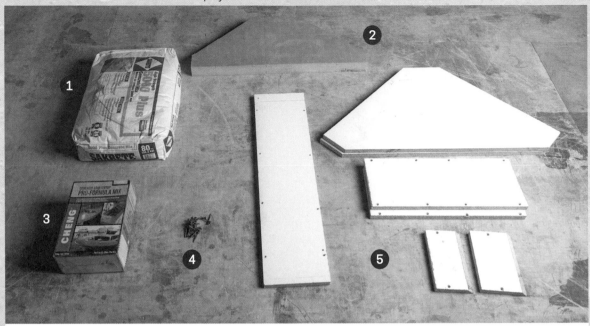

1. Sakrete 5000 Plus Concrete Mix

2. Polystyrene foam

3. Cheng Pro-Formula Mix

4. Screws

5. Melamine

MATERIALS

- One 23¼ × 23¼-inch piece of 2-inch-thick polystyrene foam cut to the dimensions shown in the illustration

- ¾-inch melamine:

    One 7½ × 30-inch piece (for the base)

    Two 27½ × 27½-inch pieces cut to the dimensions shown in the illustration (for the walls)

    Two 7½ × 4½-inch pieces, each with the edge of one long side cut at a 45-degree angle (for the end caps)

    Two 7½ × 19½-inch pieces (one of these is for the bottom of the bike stand and the other is for the back side)

- Silicone caulk

- 1¼- or 1½-inch screws

- Bicycle cog or other small embellishment

- Rubber gloves

- Two 80-lb. bags of Sakrete 5000 Plus Concrete Mix

- Two packages of Cheng Pro-Formula (we used evergreen)

- Water

- Plastic sheet

TOOLS

- Circular saw

- Tape measure

- Pencil

- Caulking gun

- Power drill or driver

- Drum mixer or 15-gallon mixing tray and electric mixer, or a wheelbarrow and hoe

- Small bucket

- Margin trowel

- Handsaw

- 80- to 120-grit sandpaper

1 **BUILD THE FORM.** Center the long side of the foam knockout on the melamine base of the form, measuring to make sure it's centered (the knockout should be equidistant from each end and each side of the base), and adhere it to the melamine with silicone. Apply silicone around the seams of the knockout too. Once the knockout is in place, position the long sides of the wall pieces so that their ends are equidistant from each end of the base, and screw them to the base, remembering to predrill holes in the melamine. Then, attach the end cap pieces to the base and the walls, one at each end, with the 45-degree edge set flush against the base (the other edge will jut out a bit).

▼ You'll need two of these.

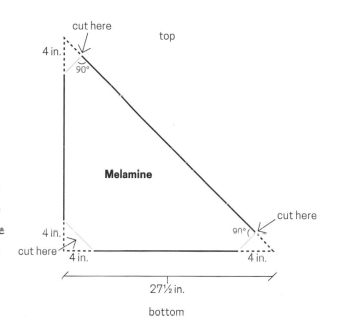

▼ You only need one of these.

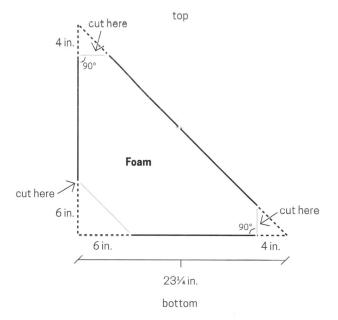

▼ Profile of the two end cap pieces.

▼ Applying silicone to the base piece of melamine.

▼ Silicone around the seam.

▼ Centering the large side pieces on the base.

2 **EMBELLISH THE BIKE STAND.** The end caps will become the top or front of the bike stand (depending on which side you stand the finished piece on) and are the perfect place to add a little something special to embellish the bike stand. We chose to stay with the bike theme, so we embedded a small bike cog in the concrete, but you can use anything you like as long as it fits. Apply a bit of silicone to the cog, and then carefully place it on the inside of one of the end caps, siliconed-side down. Finish building the form by attaching the remaining bottom and back-side pieces to the walls of the form, again predrilling the holes.

▼ Attaching the end cap pieces.

3 MIX AND CAST THE CONCRETE.

If you've made it this far, congratulations. Pour the concrete mix into the drum mixer or wheelbarrow and add water according to the directions on the Cheng Pro-Formula Mix package. Be sure that you add enough water for the concrete to be pourable; the consistency should resemble waffle batter. When the concrete is thoroughly mixed and pigmented, use a small bucket to pour it into the form until it's level with the top edges of the form. It's not imperative that you vibrate the form for this project, but if you want fewer bugholes, then vibrate the form a bit. The less you vibrate, the more bugholes will appear, so it's an aesthetic decision.

▼ A bicycle cog is the perfect addition.

▼ Positioning the cog on an end cap.

▼ Attaching the final pieces of the form.

▼ Pouring the mix into the form.

▼ Cleaning up a bit before covering it with a plastic sheet.

4 **COVER THE FORM** loosely with plastic and let it sit overnight on a flat surface to cure.

5 **DEMOLD AND PROCESS.** Remove the screws and carefully pry off the melamine with a margin trowel. Then, dig out the foam knockout. Because of the narrow space you'll be working in, digging out the knockout will take some time. A handsaw is helpful because of its reach, but feel free to use any tool you find helpful. We used a margin trowel to start and then switched to a handsaw. Once you've removed the knockout, lightly sand the edges of the concrete if you like.

▼ Removing the melamine.

▼ Digging out the foam knockout.

▲ The piece has wonderful texture and bugholes. The bike
stand can be positioned with the cog at the front or on top.

▲ The clean design of this bench combined with its sophisticated finish makes a stunning piece for a garden.

SIMPLE BENCH
RAW CONCRETE WITH ACID STAIN

This appealing garden bench features a two-tone acid-stain spray technique that creates a mottled and layered effect. Like the Cast-in-Place Side Table, this project calls for a troweling technique to bring out a natural burnished finish in the concrete. More than any other process in casting concrete, the troweled finish reveals the hand of the maker and celebrates concrete as a craft.

The bench has a simple design but a complicated form—the exterior is shaped like a rectangular box but the interior pieces of the form shape the legs and seat. It measures 36 × 16 × 18 inches and has a handle inset on each side.

▼ Some of the materials needed for this project.

1. Melamine

2. Sakrete 5000 Plus Concrete Mix

3. Tape

4. Acid stain

5. Polystyrene foam

6. Clean spray bottles

MATERIALS

- ¾-inch melamine:

  Two 18¾ × 36-inch pieces (for the sides of the outer form)

  Two 18¾ × 17½-inch pieces (for the ends of the outer form)

  Two 3 × 16-inch pieces (for the bottom of the legs of the inner form)

  Two 16 × 15¾-inch pieces (for the legs of the inner form)

  One 28½ × 16-inch piece (for the bench seat of the inner form)

- 1½-inch screws
- Packing tape
- Two 4 × 1½ × 1-inch pieces of polystyrene foam
- Silicone caulk
- Rubber gloves
- Four 80-lb. bags of Sakrete 5000 Plus Concrete Mix
- Water

- Two 45-inch lengths of masonry ladder wire
- Sheet plastic
- Two acid stains (we used walnut and weathered wheat)

TOOLS

- Table saw or circular saw
- Power drill or driver and bit
- Small 3-inch-wide piece of wood
- Caulking gun
- Drum mixer or wheelbarrow and hoe
- Hammer or orbital sander
- 24-inch-long screed
- Resin or wood trowel
- Steel trowel
- Margin trowel
- 80- to 120-grit sandpaper
- Two spray bottles
- Clean rags, brush, or sponge

1 **BUILD THE FORM.** Begin by building the outer part of the form, which will look like a rectangular box that doesn't have a top or bottom. Remember to predrill the screw holes to ensure a tight fit and solid construction. Screw the two 18¾ × 36-inch side pieces to the two 18¾ × 17½-inch end pieces to make the box. Next, assemble the inner part of the form. Set the outer form on its side and screw the two 3 × 16-inch pieces to the bottom corners; these are the part of the form that makes the legs of the bench (they'll be the bottom surface of the legs). Once the 3 × 16-inch pieces are secured, attach the 16 × 15¾-inch pieces to the 3 × 16-inch pieces.

▼ Screwing together the form.

▼ The outer form.

▼ Attaching the 3-inch strips to the bottom corners.

▼ Placing the inner form walls.

▼ Using a spacer block to make sure the legs are correctly positioned.

▼ The inner walls of the form in place. They'll form the legs of the bench.

Use a small 3-inch spacer block as a guide to keep the inside pieces parallel with the outside pieces. The inside pieces will frame the legs of the bench and should be secured with screws drilled through the outer form. Dry fit the inside pieces first, mark their placement, and use the marks to guide you as you predrill the holes. This helps prevent misplacing a screw and ruining the form. Complete the inner form by positioning the 28½ × 16-inch piece between the two inner 16 × 15¾-inch pieces and screwing it in place through the outside of the form.

Then, waterproof the exposed edges of melamine by running packing tape along them. This is an important step: if the exposed edges are not taped, water from the mix will cause the melamine to swell, creating uneven areas (some thick, some thin) in the concrete while it's curing that will alter the overall shape of the form.

Next, attach the foam knockouts. Center a knockout inside each of the ends of the outer form about 3 inches from the top edge and silicone it into place. The knockouts create the handles that are inset on each side of the bench. Silicone the edges of the form wherever you can to ease the edges and waterproof the form.

2 **MIX THE CONCRETE.** Because of the size of this project, we opted to use a drum mixer. Pour the concrete into the mixer, add water, and mix until the cement has a consistency that resembles chunky waffle batter and is easily poured but not runny.

▼ Attaching the bench seat to the inner form.

▼ Taping the melamine edge.

▼ Positioning the knockouts that create the inset handles.

▼ Pouring the legs first.

3 **CAST THE CONCRETE.** Pour the concrete into the form, filling up the legs first. Vibrate the form by hand using a hammer or other device such as an orbital sander as you fill the legs to minimize air pockets and create a smooth finish. Once the legs are full, pour a 1-inch-thick layer of concrete across the bench seat. Bend both ends of the pieces of ladder wire at a 90-degree angle and lay the pieces across the concrete, inserting the bent ends into the cast legs. The ladder wire should be positioned about 2 to 3 inches from the sides of the form.

▼ Inserting the ladder wire into the legs.

▼ Positioning the two pieces of masonry ladder wire near the top.

Once the ladder wire is placed, continue pouring in the concrete, filling the form to the top, and vibrating the form to help the mix consolidate. Use the screed to make the surface of the concrete flat, using the top edges of the form as a guide. Then fill in any low spots as needed, and use the resin or wood trowel to smooth the surface. The proper way to use a float or trowel is to slightly lift the leading edge as you move across the surface. This prevents any gouging or digging into the surface.

▼ Filling and screeding the top.

▼ Floating after screeding.

▼ Smoothing with a resin float.

▼ Proper form using steel float.

▼ Beginning to burnish the surface.

4 **TROWEL THE CONCRETE.** This is the point in the project where it is important to be patient and not rush the process. Let the concrete cure until it is stiff to the touch—this can take anywhere from 20 minutes to 2 hours depending on a number of factors, such as the amount of water used in the mix and the weather. Once the concrete has stiffened, trowel it again with the resin or wood float. Troweling the concrete again pushes the aggregate down and brings a workable cream to the surface. Trowel until the surface is clean and flat again and let it sit for another 20 minutes or so. Next, use the steel trowel to smooth the surface. At this point you can bear down on the trowel to burnish the surface, bringing out the beauty and uniqueness of your work.

▼ Removing the form.

5 **TENT THE FORM WITH PLASTIC.** Don't let the plastic touch the surface of the concrete—it can discolor the surface if it sits directly on the finished surface. Let the form cure for a couple of days before demolding.

▼ Preparing the surface for staining.

6 **DEMOLD AND PROCESS.** Remove the screws and carefully pull off the melamine form. The concrete will be relatively fresh and not fully cured yet, so take special care while removing the form—the leverage that's applied to the corners of the bench while you're pulling apart the form can easily cause it to crack (trust us—we have experience with this). Dig out the foam knockouts from the inset handles. Once the form and knockouts are removed, lightly sand the corners and edges of the bench. Do not aggressively sand the troweled top, because heavy sanding can remove or damage the beautiful burnished surface you worked so hard on. Wipe down the bench to remove any dust and to prepare the surface for acid staining.

7 **APPLY THE ACID STAIN.** Pour the stains into spray bottles. Begin by spraying one part of the bench with one acid stain and then another part of the bench with the other stain. Work from one end to the other, alternating the stains— this will give the bench a dappled, mottled look. Be sure to saturate the concrete, allowing it to absorb the stain as you work your way around the bench. Let the stain completely dry on the surface and then wash the remaining residue off with a damp sponge, rag, or soft brush. Once the stain dries, the bench is finished and ready to be placed under your favorite tree.

▼ Alternating the acid stains to achieve a mottled effect.

▼ Covering the entire surface of the bench.

▼ Careful troweling results in a deep burnished surface.

▲ A stylish birdhouse is made from two concrete pieces.

MODERN BIRDHOUSE
INTEGRAL COLOR FOR BRILLIANT WHITE

This charming birdhouse provides an elegant point of interest in a garden and demonstrates how to get a beautiful brilliant white by adding white pigment to white Portland cement. This is a color technique that is underutilized in color concrete projects, so we feel it's a nice addition to anyone's skill set.

By using a high-strength mix design, you'll be able to make a project that is lightweight and delicate and will hold up to the elements. The birdhouse consists of two parts, so you'll be casting concrete into two forms: one for the roof and one for the body. We used a small trash can and a plastic container salvaged from a recycling bin for the form for the body of the house.

The birdhouse measures $7\frac{1}{4} \times 7\frac{1}{4} \times 12$ inches and can be easily taken apart for cleaning. The two forms for this project are among the most challenging in this book. They're very detailed, so we strongly recommend reading and reviewing all the steps before you begin to work.

▼ Some of the materials needed for this project.

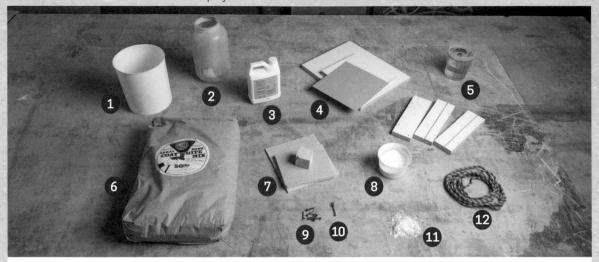

1. Small trash can
2. Small container
3. Water reducer
4. Melamine and laminate
5. Water
6. Buddy Rhodes Bone White Spray Coat
7. Polystyrene foam
8. Pigment
9. Screws
10. Bolt with washers and nuts
11. PVA fibers
12. Rope

MATERIALS

- Plastic cylinder with a 7¼-inch diameter
- Plastic cylinder with a 6-inch diameter
- Polystyrene foam:

    One ½ × 10 × 10-inch piece (for the house form)

    One ¼ × 12 × 12-inch piece (for the roof form)

    One ½ × 2 × 2-inch piece (for the bird hole knockout)

- Silicone caulk
- ¾-inch melamine:

    One 9 × 9-inch piece (for the base of the roof form)

    Three 9¾ × 3-inch pieces (for the sides of the roof form)

    One 12 × 12-inch piece (for the base of the house form)

- 1¼-inch screws
- 9 × 9½-inch piece of laminate
- 6-inch length of ⅜-inch-wide rubber tubing
- Two 2-inch long bolts with washers and nuts
- Rubber gloves
- Approximately ¼ of a 50-lb. bag of Buddy Rhodes Bone White Spray Coat

- Water
- Water reducer
- Pigment (we used titanium white, from Blue Concrete)
- PVA fibers
- Rope to hang the birdhouse (the width of the rope needs to fit through the plastic tubing)
- Plastic sheet

TOOLS

- Box cutter or carpenter's knife
- Pencil or felt marker
- 80- to 120-grit sandpaper
- Table saw or circular saw
- Caulking gun
- Power drill or driver
- Small bucket, plastic container, or bowl
- Mixing paddle
- Kitchen scale
- Large bucket
- Margin trowel

1 **PREPARE THE PARTS OF THE FORM.** When the form is assembled, there will be a gap of a little more than ½ inch between the walls of the cylinders. Concrete is poured into the gap, forming the wall of the birdhouse. Cut the two cylinders to a height of 7⅜ inches, taking care to keep the cuts square to the sides and completely level across. Once the cylinders are cut, trace the diameter of the smaller cylinder onto the ½-inch-thick piece of foam, and trace the diameter of the larger cylinder onto the ¼-inch-thick piece of foam. Cut out both circles using a box cutter or a carpenter's knife, but cut out the larger circle about ⅛ inch bigger than the tracing you made (measure and draw a second circle to guide you if necessary).

▼ Cutting the outer form (the small trash can).

▼ Cutting the inner form (the recycled container).

▼ Tracing the inner form onto ½-inch-thick foam.

▼ Tracing the outer form onto ¼-inch-thick foam.

▼ Assembling the form. The foam circle is adhered to the melamine.

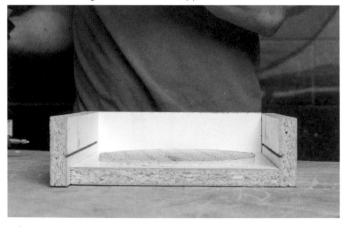

▼ The two grooved sides are opposite each other in the form.

Next, make the knockout for the bird hole by cutting a circle of approximately 1⅜ inches in diameter from the 2 × 2-inch piece of foam. Sand the two flat sides of the circle so that it fits snugly in between the curved walls of the forms.

Last, cut a groove down the length of the long side of two of the 9¾ × 3-inch pieces of melamine about 1¼ inches from the edge that will be the bottom of the form. These two pieces will be opposite each other in the form, and once the form is assembled, the groove will hold the piece of laminate in place, giving it a slight arch.

2 ASSEMBLE THE FORM FOR THE ROOF. Attach the larger foam circle to the center of the 9 × 9-inch piece of melamine using silicone. Then, screw the sides of the form to the base, placing the two grooved pieces opposite each other. Once the sides are attached, silicone the interior seams to prevent leaking. Slide the piece of laminate into the grooved pieces and silicone it into place. The final step in assembling the form is to drill a ⅜-inch hole through the laminate and insert a 4-inch piece of plastic tubing; push the tubing through the laminate until it touches the foam circle. You may need to seal around the tube with silicone and let the silicone cure for 30 minutes.

3 ASSEMBLE THE FORM FOR THE HOUSE.

First, prepare the smaller cylinder. Adhere the ½-inch foam circle onto one end of the smaller cylinder with silicone. The foam circle should sit inside the cylinder and be flush with the edge. This will be the top end of the form. Drill a hole in the center of the ½-inch-thick foam and insert a 2-inch piece of plastic tubing. Then, adhere the round foam knockout for the bird hole to the cylinder about 1½ inches from the bottom edge, and push a bolt through it. (Once the larger cylinder is added to the form, the bolt will keep the two cylinders stable and maintain an even wall thickness.)

▼ The laminate is held in place by the grooves, and the seams are being sealed with silicone.

▼ Positioning the rubber tube.

▼ Adhering the foam circle into the inner form with silicone.

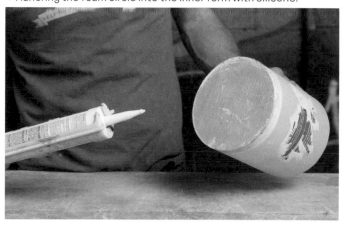

▼ The foam knockout for the bird hole with the bolt in place.

▼ The perch installed in the outer form.

▼ The rubber tube installed.

Next, prepare the larger cylinder. Drill a small hole through the larger cylinder in the center of the corresponding position of the bird hole on the smaller cylinder. Now drill another small hole through the larger cylinder 2⅛ inches below the first hole (this hole is for the bolt that acts a perch). Insert a 2-inch bolt into the lower hole and screw one nut onto the bolt on the inside of the cylinder and one bolt onto the screw on the outside of the cylinder. The bolt will remain embedded in the concrete wall and will act as the perch for the birdhouse.

Silicone the open end of the smaller cylinder to the 12 × 12-inch piece of melamine. Once the silicone is dry, center the larger cylinder over the smaller; you will need to flex the larger cylinder to fit over the bolt in the smaller cylinder, lining up the two spots where the bird hole is. Once you are satisfied that everything is lined up, silicone the outer cylinder to the melamine.

▼ Adhering the inner form to the melamine with silicone.

4 **MIX THE CONCRETE.** The mix for this project is more advanced to give us a finished product that is lighter and stronger than a normal off-the-shelf bagged mix. Because this is a custom mix, use a kitchen scale to measure out the ingredients to the gram. If you've used cylinders that are not the same size as called for in this project, increase or decrease the ingredients listed here as needed, but keep the ratio of the concrete mix the same.

- 1600 grams of Buddy Rhodes Bone White Spray Coat
- 400 grams of water
- 10 grams of water reducer
- 16 grams of white pigment
- 2 grams of PVA fibers

▼ Adding the PVA fibers to the concrete mix.

▼ Mixing the concrete with a drill and mixing paddle.

▼ The paddle used for mixing.

▼ Filling the forms with concrete.

▼ Smoothing the concrete with a trowel.

Carefully measure the ingredients into the bucket or bowl and mix until you have a consistency similar to pancake batter. Pour the mix into the forms. As you fill the forms, vibrate them by hand to release any air trapped in the form. When the forms are full, smooth the concrete with a margin trowel for a nice finish.

5 COVER THE FORMS loosely with plastic and let them sit overnight on a flat surface to cure.

▼ Demolding the roof.

6 DEMOLD THE FORMS. Remove the screws in the roof form and carefully pry off the sides using a margin trowel. Now remove the foam using a knife and/or margin trowel. For the body of the house you will need to cut the inner and outer plastic forms. Take care doing this so that you do not cut into the concrete surface. Also remove the foam from the bird hole and the plastic tubing from the bottom. As usual, you may want to sand the edges a bit with 80- to 120-grit sandpaper.

▼ Carefully removing the outer form.

7 ASSEMBLE THE BIRDHOUSE. Tie a solid knot in one end of the rope and thread it through the hole in the bottom of the birdhouse and then through the roof. Carefully seat the birdhouse into the recessed area in the roof.

▲ The two pieces assembled.

METRIC CONVERSIONS

INCHES	CENTIMETERS
1/10	0.3
1/6	0.4
1/4	0.6
1/3	0.8
1/2	1.3
3/4	1.9
1	2.5
2	5.1
3	7.6
4	10
5	13
6	15
7	18
8	20
9	23
10	25

FEET	METERS
1	0.3
2	0.6
3	0.9
4	1.2
5	1.5
6	1.8
7	2.1
8	2.4
9	2.7
10	3

OUNCES	GRAMS
0.04	1
0.07	2
0.11	3
0.14	4
0.18	5
0.21	6
0.25	7
0.28	8
0.32	9
0.35	10
14.11	400
56.44	1600

RESOURCES

AMERICAN FIRE GLASS

americanfireglass.com

This is an online resource for fire pit installation kits and burners. You can order online or find a dealer close to your location. They also sell fire glass to cover the burner.

BLUE CONCRETE

blueconcrete.com

An online store dedicated to making concrete better. They sell raw materials for making high-performance concrete such as cements, aggregates, pozzolans, admixtures, color, equipment, and reinforcement. They can match any shade on the Benjamin Moore color wheel.

BUDDY RHODES CONCRETE PRODUCTS

buddyrhodes.com

A pioneer in the decorative concrete industry for more than 30 years, Buddy Rhodes developed a mix design that came to market in 2004. Today the company sells a complete product line that makes using concrete easier. They sell high-performance bagged mixes, reinforcement, sealers, molds, equipment, and pigments. Their products are available online and at numerous dealer locations.

CHENG DESIGN

concreteexchange.com

An innovator in the decorative concrete industry, Fu-Tung Cheng developed an easy way to take locally bagged commercial-grade mixes sold at home-improvement stores and make a higher-performance and colored concrete by adding a package of Cheng Pro-Formula Mix. They sell concrete mixes, sealers, form supplies, tools, and equipment. Their products are available online.

DIAMOND TOOLS

If you wish to step it up a notch, diamond tooling is a great way to refine and finish concrete and take it to the next level. When you are ready to take that next step, check out the websites for Buddy Rhodes, Cheng Design, and Applied Diamond Tools (**toolocity.com**).

QUIKRETE CEMENT & CONCRETE PRODUCTS
quikrete.com

Quikrete is one of the most easily accessible concrete bagged mixes available; find Quikrete products at most home-improvement stores.

SAKRETE
sakrete.com

This is another one of the most easily accessible concrete bagged mixes available. Their products are sold at most large home-improvement stores.

SET IN STONE SUPPLY
concretedesignhouse.com

Our online store is a resource for fine concrete craft as well as materials for anyone who wants to explore the craft. Check out concretecaster.com for training opportunities and design inspiration.

HOME-IMPROVEMENT STORES: LOWE'S, HOME DEPOT, ACE HARDWARE, TRUE VALUE

These stores have been a staple in creating the projects in this book. We purchased all the off-the-shelf commercial-grade concrete mixes for this book at these stores. Form material, safety gear, and other miscellaneous supplies are also easily sourced from them as well as most of the tools needed for the projects in this book.

CRAFT STORES: MICHAELS, HOME GOODS, HOBBY LOBBY, JOANN FABRIC AND CRAFT STORES

These stores provided a lot of the smaller details that went into making many of the projects in this book. Smaller craft-type items like stencils, cardboard tubes, and premade shapes (such as letters and numbers) can be sourced from these stores. They are great places to search for project inspiration.

LOCAL RESOURCES

Don't forget to shop locally and support your community. There are all kinds of craftsmen and craftswomen who may be willing to help and supply some of the materials you need. Consider welding shops, woodshops, thrift stores, nurseries, and garden centers. Try local cabinet and millwork shops for form materials. The local recycling center can be a great resource for all kinds of free plastic containers and miscellaneous form materials.

ACKNOWLEDGMENTS

WE GRATEFULLY THANK—

ALL THE GUYS AND GALS AT THE SIS SHOP:

Justin

Staj

Lindsay

Sam

ALL THE PEOPLE IN OUR INDUSTRY WHO HAVE HELPED AND ENCOURAGED US DURING THE WRITING PROCESS:

Buddy

Jeremy

David

OUR FAMILY AND TEACHERS AND FRIENDS:

Nathan's grandfather for first encouraging the need to make and create

Our wives who continually support us and who we get to bounce ideas off of

Our kids who we hope will one day find joy in making

Nathan's parents for their support and letting us shoot our projects in their garden

The Meyers family who let us rearrange their garden to fit our concrete in it

INDEX

◄ **Nathan Smith** has a BBA in business management with an emphasis in entrepreneurship. He started his journey with concrete in the form of countertops for his own home. The material was fascinating and the medium was too much to resist. Since its formation in 2007, Set in Stone has slowly assembled a team of talented and creative individuals. They all consider themselves a part of a concrete evolution, using the seemingly limitless material to enrich lives ultimately through the creative process. He resides in Chattanooga, Tennessee. He feels at home in the shop, on a bike in the woods, and especially hanging out with his family.

◄ **Michael Snyder** is an artisan craftsman with a background in sculpture and carpentry. He works at Set in Stone, a concrete design company with a focus on making beautiful useful objects. He lives in Chattanooga, Tennessee.

◄ **Charles Coleman** is a photographer based in Chattanooga, Tennessee, with over nine years in the field. His works are fostered from a desire to express stories through mediums ranging from tintype photography to video documentary. Visit charlescolemanphotography.com for more information.